Journey of a Lifetime

Journey of a Lifetime

Kathryn Acheson Chartrand

Archway Publishing books may be ordered through booksellers or by contacting:

Archway Publishing
1663 Liberty Drive
Bloomington, IN 47403
www.archwaypublishing.com
844-669-3957

ISBN: 978-1-6657-5388-3 (sc)
ISBN: 978-1-6657-5389-0 (e)

Library of Congress Control Number: 2023923096

Print information available on the last page.

Archway Publishing rev. date: 11/29/2023

Prologue by Kathy

In June, 1972, after three years of teaching in a Quebec elementary school, I resigned. I had decided I did not want to teach after all. Don't get me wrong! I loved the students and education, but I was only 19 when I started to teach and really excited about opening up young minds to education both in and out of the classroom. It didn't take me long to realize that I was too excited; my Grade 2 kids picked up on it, and there were times I truly felt I had lost control; I needed to become strict. Not what I wanted! Also, looking back on it now, I think I was a perfectionist. I sincerely wanted to be the best I could be for my class. However, perfect is not possible, so Parent/Teacher Interviews made me really nervous. Any criticism left me questioning my worth as a teacher. I felt inadequate, so I left. I wanted to get my Bachelor of Arts Degree and pursue another career even though, at that time, I had no idea what that career might be. I applied and was accepted at Ryerson University in Toronto.

In August, of '72, my parents and I travelled to Toronto so I could secure a job and a place to stay while pursuing my studies. It was such a successful trip! I was hired during my first interview. When university started, in September, I was to begin working, part time, for Eaton's, a large department store that closed in 1999. Not only did the store manager agree to schedule my hours around my classes, but she even offered me low rent, sharing an apartment with her sister. All I had to do was go home, pack up my necessities, return to T.O., my new home, and begin my life as a working student. The thing is, that's not how it turned out at all! On our way back home to Montreal, as we passed Cornwall, an Ontario city about 45 minutes west of Montreal, I presented my parents with an alternative plan.

"Mom, Dad, I know everything is set for me in Toronto, but do you think we could make a little detour? I'd like to see if there happens to be a university in Cornwall." Now, at that time, Cornwall was a fairly small, industrial city of about 46,000 people. The likelihood of finding a university in a city of that size was extremely remote. However, Dad did as I asked, and we went to investigate. "Google" might have been someone's dream for the future, but in 1972 the city phone book served us well. To my happy surprise, there was a university! A branch of the University of Ottawa was located in Cornwall. We found the address of the administration office, I went in, presented my Teaching Credentials, my High School transcripts, and stated that I had been accepted at Ryerson but would prefer to attend classes through the University of Ottawa, and I was in! My life was about to change!

Kathy

Dad worked for Bell Canada, and in 1972 his position was located in Montreal. Being a uni-lingual English businessman, he was not too happy about the Quebec politics of the day. Therefore, he bought a farm near the small village of North Lancaster, Ontario, which is located very close to the Quebec/Ontario border, northeast of Cornwall. My parents were not intending to move into it right away, but when I discovered that Cornwall housed a branch of the University of Ottawa, I kind of hurried things along and had us moving in by Labour Day Weekend. Dad, Mom, a couple of my sisters, and I left Montreal for rural life on a farm, in an unfamiliar area. I had registered at the University just a few days before we made our move, and in October, 1972, I began working toward my Bachelor of Arts Degree in Psychology.

My soon-to-be husband, Luc, had also registered at U of O. Once we met, our fast-track friendship, courtship, and marriage were in play. We had our first date in November and were married April 23rd, 1973, about 6 months after our first "Hello!" I was twenty-three, and he was twenty-one. You may wonder why we were in such a hurry. Well, I have to admit that in those days, at twenty-three years of age, motherhood was on my mind, but Luc was just twenty-one, and he was not ready. However, our rush to the altar was actually for a different reason. Let me explain.

Luc

From my birth until I met Luc, my family had moved every few years between Montreal and Toronto. Luc's family, on the other hand, had settled in Cornwall where his dad worked at the Howard Smith Paper Mill. Luc had four older siblings. When he was about twelve, his mom was diagnosed with a serious brain tumour. The doctor was only able to remove part of it, so they all knew her prognosis was terminal. What they didn't know was for how long she might survive. Frequently, Luc's dad drove his mom to the Montreal Neurological Institute for treatment. Then,when Luc was about thirteen, his seventeen-year-old brother, one evening, while riding home on a bicycle from his girlfriend's house, was seriously injured when he was hit by a drunk driver. He was rushed to the hospital where he remained, for weeks, in a coma. Once he did wake up, he was never the same. He sustained severe physical and brain damage. He became a paraplegic. His speech, mental processes and motor skills were seriously altered; he was extremely difficult to understand. He was placed in a full care facility. Then, one morning, when Luc was sixteen, his dad said he wasn't feeling too well and asked Luc if he would drive him to the hospital. He did, dropped him off, and his dad said he would call home when he needed to be picked up. He never called. The hospital contacted them to inform his mom that Mr. Chartrand had passed away due to a massive thrombosis of the heart. Now Luc's three older sisters were already established in their own lives, all married or about to, and building their families, so sixteen-year-old Luc became the primary caregiver of both his mom and his brother.

Luc was determined to get a higher education, so in 1971/72 he attended Teachers' College in Ottawa and would hitchhike back to Cornwall on the weekends. He had to take his mom to frequent neurological appointments in Montreal and accompany her on visits with his brother at his care facility. Following his year at Teacher's College, Luc realized he needed to remain closer to home, so Cornwall's university branch served as his educational base. He was living with and caring for his mom, in an apartment, when we met in the cafeteria of the high school that housed the university courses. We both wanted his mom to be present at our wedding, but her health was deteriorating, so we made some quick decisions, and she was able to attend. Sadly, she did pass away a few months later.

Once I got to know him, and we began to plan a life together, I realized that my desire to become a parent quickly was not nearly as important as Luc's need to escape responsibility for a while. We decided we would start our family once we were out of apartments and into our own home.

Our Cautionary Tale

I had returned to school to receive an education that would lead me in a direction other than teaching, but when Luc and I got married, neither one of us had a permanent, full time job. We each had temporary positions, I at The Department of Supply and Services for the Federal Government, and Luc for the Federal Government as well, at the local Unemployment Insurance Office. Initially we lived in a tiny basement apartment with only one window, so, by the summer of 1973, we had to figure out what to do. Reluctantly, I put my name on the list of substitute teachers with both the Catholic and Public school boards and, from September to December, I travelled throughout the Cornwall area from school to school. Meanwhile, Luc supply-taught as well and took on various part-time jobs.

In the Fall of '73, Dad was unexpectedly transferred to Ottawa, for the first time in his career. In preference to commuting daily, he and Mom decided to rent a place in Ottawa and return to the farm on weekends. Because there were animals at the farm who needed care, Luc and I took over for them...no rent, only car concerns. As time passed, Luc became increasingly uncomfortable, especially on weekends when the parents were home, for he did not really know where his duties began and ended. As soon as Dad had bought the farm he brought in cows and horses. During the week, Luc had his methods of caring for the animals and barn, but when Dad returned, he had his own way, thus the discomfort.

In January, 1974, I secured a half-time teaching position in Cornwall, and Luc, around that time, found a full-time job working with the Cornwall Physically Disabled and Handicapped Club of which his brother was a member. For a few months, everything went well. We were able to save enough money to put a deposit on a new car: a gorgeous, white Camaro; with both of us working, and living for free, we could easily afford it. Unfortunately, Luc did not like living in my parents' home, so in the spring we committed to an apartment in Cornwall, commencing in September. Still, both of us were working, so, okay.

One Friday night, just before going out with friends, my husband informed me that he hated his job and had quit. Now we could not afford both a car and the apartment, so we had to trade the car back in to the dealership. However, that very evening, while out with our buddies, we got into an accident which really damaged the front end of the vehicle. Oh Boy! Dollars lost! That night I was not a happy camper (as the saying goes)!

We bought a used car and moved into our apartment, another basement but this time we had nice big windows. I continued teaching, and Luc, never a slouch, worked at various jobs, between supply-teaching positions. Although he had attended Teachers' College before I met him, Luc had not passed one of the courses. He missed out by a percentage or two; he believed the professor had not liked him, maybe because he had been a bit mouthy? So, he could not be officially hired by the school board; they could, however, continue calling on him as a substitute.

One day, after a couple of years, as Luc bounced from pillar to post, we sat down and discussed the future. Like it or not, it appeared that I was "stuck" in Teaching...it has to be about money sometimes. But what did Luc want to do? He said he really wanted to be a teacher. We decided we needed to find a way. He made an appointment with the Dean of the Faculty of Education for the University of Ottawa. He reviewed Luc's results from the course he had failed, explained that it was about French Grammar, and that the only way the Faculty could override these results would be if Luc were willing to attend and pass a university grammar course provided on campus. For months, through good and wicked weather, Luc travelled to Ottawa, twice weekly, in pursuit of final success. He achieved it, with great marks, and received his teaching certification. We were both so pleased! In fact, I think we might even have cried a little bit; anyway, I'm sure I did!

Now I would like to say that all went well once we both had teaching jobs, but I can't. You see, in the '70s, French Immersion was becoming popular, and instead of sending children to "French" schools, a lot of parents were opting for "French Immersion." I guess, if Luc had wanted to become a "French as a Second Language" teacher, for the English board, his job might have been secured. But his heart and his experience had been with the French board, and, at the time, there was a position waiting for him. The problem was, however, that each year, for maybe the next seven, his position became redundant; mine did not. I kept teaching, and each June, Luc received his letter of termination. Eventually, we had to accept our situation and plan our lives in spite of it.

In the summer of 1974, Luc and I decided to take a trip to Toronto to visit the CNE (Canadian National Exhibition). We were already thinking about getting out of apartment living and into home ownership, so we were drawn to a pavilion catering to home construction and renovation. Right in the centre of the massive arena was a two-story log house. It was gorgeous! We spoke with the people responsible and learned how we could have one of these beauties delivered and erected on our own lot. Now the display model was, of course, a dream house, so there was no way we could afford a building of this size. However, we were assured that the company,

"Four Seasons Log Homes," which was located in Parry Sound, Ontario, would custom-build. We collected all the information we could then went home to talk about the possibilities and make a decision. We knew we would first have to save for a down payment. I was in charge of the finances at that time, so saving became my task and goal.

A couple of months later, following an outing with his sister, Lucie, Luc informed me that they had found adjacent lots on which both of our families could build. He had committed to buying a corner lot, for $2,750, on a main county road in St. Andrews West, a village just north of Cornwall. Each measured 105' x 150', the perfect size for a country lot because we were going to have to provide our own water and sewage; city services did not extend to St Andrews. Oh my! It is here where I will make an apology for measurement terminology. You see, at that time, we were still talking Imperial Measure, not yet Metric.

I had saved $1,000, so Luc put that down on the land, and we paid off the balance over the following year. In the Fall of 1975, we began searching for a bank that would lend us money for our mortgage. We faced a few problems. We were just beginning to build seniority with our respective school boards, and, although we were both still pursuing our higher education, neither of us had yet earned our university degrees. We could only afford to educate one of us at-a-time, and since I would likely, at some point, be going on Maternity Leave(s) and losing income, we decided Luc's degree was more important at that time; I would work at mine, but, as it turned out, much more slowly. However, due to this fact: minimal experience and education, our incomes were near the bottom of the salary grids, around $10,000 each. In addition, since my job was the permanent one, and I would likely be bearing children in the near future, investing in us would be a bit risky for any financial institution. To further complicate matters, we were building an unusual house outside of the city limits. A couple of banks wouldn't even consider us, and others said they would agree if we were to put 25% down on the mortgage; we could not. We finally found the Provincial Bank, called the National Bank these days. They would lend us a max of $30,000; they accepted the land as equivalent to a 5% down payment but insisted upon CMHC (Canada Mortgage and Housing Commission) approval. The five-year, fixed interest rate on the mortgage, was 11 3/4%, amortized over 25 years.

Having researched the prices of the log houses in the "Four Seasons Log Homes" catalogue, we knew we would have to design our own floor plan. I drew an uneducated plan for a three-bedroom bungalow of 1,000 square feet; we presented it to the company for approval. My floor plan and all the construction and material stipulations were discussed, accepted, and approved. Construction was to begin in Spring, 1976.

Throughout the winter of '75/'76 we received communication from the construction company: the blueprints, the contract which included everything we had discussed as part of our package, a list of preparations we would have to have completed before they would deliver the wood, and a payment schedule. Because a building crew would be arriving from the Parry Sound area, setting up their trailer, and only leaving once the job was done, all preliminaries had to be completed before their arrival.

I won't bore you with some of the details, especially since I have forgotten many of them. However, just remember, everything costs, and we knew nothing...talk about "learn as you go!" We certainly did.

* * *

Where we were situated in St. Andrews, the well was to be located at the back of the house and the septic system at the front. This was in order to keep the septic system from contaminating the well water. No problem, in early Spring, 1976, we called the local well drilling company, "Roy's." Remember that name because I will be using it often! The first thing he asked was where we wanted our well. All we said was "...at the back." He wanted to know where, specifically; we had no idea. We told him we figured he would know where to drill since drilling the local wells was what he did on a daily basis. I thought water was everywhere; drill down, hit some, and voilà... water! Not so! He said St. Andrews was known for being dry. Now this was so hard to believe because, behind the houses across the road from us, flowed the very busy Raisin River which never dries up. However, as we found out, geologically speaking, the river had nothing to do with the water table on our side of the road.

Roy unscientifically calculated where our neighbours' water veins ran and drilled, approximately, along that line. Unfortunately, the results produced very little water. However, we were, legally and financially, committed. Wood was arriving and construction was to begin soon, so we had to find a solution. For a well to be approved, water had to flow into the house at a rate of at least four gallons per minute. Ours did not. Roy reported that it did but suggested that, in order to make his report true, he could dig a much larger hole, around the drilled well, from ground surface to the bedrock, and drop two large concrete cauldrons into the hole, one on top of the other; they would collect surface water which would then flow into the well. We approved, and the job got done.

When it was time to begin construction on the basement, we found out that our land was too low. Water had to run away from the house to the ditches and not the other way around. No one wants a flooded basement. Thus arrived tons and tons of fill which had to be levelled, compacted and graded. The septic system also had to fit into the front yard plan. A septic system consisted of a large holding tank for household drainage, a pipe leading from the house to the tank, another one, perpendicular to the tank, attached to numerous pipes that ran, perpendicularly from it, out into the front section of the property, where the dissolved waste would be distributed. This is called a tile bed. There were specifics dictating size of tank, distance from house, and depth of both the tank and the tile bed. We trusted that all was correct, and weekly, an inspector from CMHC came by to check everything out, so we felt confident. Many unforeseen problems were arising, not covered by CMHC or the bank, so we were having to pay a lot out of pocket. Painful!

One fine day the wood arrived. The house was to be of double, interlocking log construction. Each piece measured approximately 4"x6" and was numbered; it was like a puzzle. The whole house was to be completed within a few weeks. A couple of weeks after the wood arrived, the crew showed up with their trailer and started building our first home.

It was fascinating! Nowhere in our area had there been such a structure. Passers-by would stop to watch, not only because it was unique, but also because it was going up so quickly! This became a problem. You see, unlike conventional homes which consist of a frame, exterior walls, insulation, a vapour barrier, and inner walls, each being constructed and/or installed in a specific order, our double log walls were rising together, so the building inspector, with his once-a-week visits, couldn't keep up. At one point, when the contractors had built beyond what he had intended to inspect, he had to be talked out of making them tear down what they had done.

Approvals for monetary disbursements were not arriving fast

enough. One week the inspector handed us a list of items we had to have completed before he would approve any further money. The projects included the front and back decks and a driveway, all of which were out of the purview of the "home" construction. We had no cash or savings. Our bank could not lend us anything outside of the disbursements, and because our incomes were fairly low, no other bank would approve us for a loan.

I called my dad, told him our situation, and asked him if he could lend us $4,000 to do what needed to be done. In his very business-like manner he said he would lend us the money "...at the going rate." I was devastated, so hurt. I had cost him so little in my life...no schooling or tuition fees, maybe a few textbooks, not even clothes; I had been buying my own, through my summer jobs, since I was about 15. It wasn't that we hadn't intended to pay interest on the loan, we had every intention of paying back the principle and more; it was how he talked to me, not like a daughter at all and "the going rate"... really? Anyway, I cried for a long time. When I had calmed down, I called Mom. Around a year before this, she had returned to work, for the first time since she and Dad had married. I explained our situation to her and asked if she could help us. She told me not to worry, she would get us the money right away...not even a mention of interest. True to her word, we had the money by that weekend. She had gone to the bank in the Federal Government building in which she worked. Initially, the lending officer wanted her husband's co-signature on the loan, but she refused, and she won. She was great! Luc and I paid her back in full within a year-and-a-half, along with a couple of extra payments. She never told us what interest she had to pay.

When our construction package arrived, in early Spring, we felt like kids opening a box of Lego...a massive, baffling puzzle. At that time we were incapable of assessing whether the total inventory aligned with our signed contract. However, once construction was nearing the end, we realized that the 2"x4" tongue-and-groove pine flooring, that had been in our contract, was missing. Because we had not had any previous experience in building any structure, let alone one so different, we had figured, maybe, the floor went on after the building was completed, on top of the plywood that had already been installed, but the pieces just weren't there. When we contacted the company, they said that they had forgotten, but because they had supplied us with plywood floors, the best they could do was send us the equivalent in 1"x4" tongue -and-groove. We learned that that would not work well as flooring since it was too thin and if something weighty were placed where tongue met groove, the wood might snap. Days later the flooring arrived; it was covered and set aside. About a year later Luc used it to build our garage.

We were not supposed to have plywood floors, but there we were, and we were left wondering what to do and how to afford floor covering. Luckily we had kept two rugs from past apartments, so we were able to cut and adjust them to fit, wall-to-wall, in two of our three bedrooms, then we had to purchase linoleum and carpets for the rest of the house. Once again, this had not been factored into our financial plan.

You know, when you embark, blindly, on such an adventure, you soon learn how ill-equipped you are for the voyage. It seemed that with every step forward we met a "road block," physical, emotional, and, mostly, financial. In our naivety, we thought buying the land, planning a very modest home, and securing a mortgage for it would be sufficient...dream come true! How wrong we were!

There were so many expenses! However, our house, once completed, all moneys disbursed, and ready for occupancy, was beautiful!

We were able to move in by late summer. We did love it; so did our families! I remember one of my sisters, as she lay on the light green carpet in our bedroom, looking up at the cathedral-style ceiling, saying, "Kath, do you ever feel like you are living in Heaven?" I smiled and confirmed that I really did feel fortunate. Hmmm! Was I?

The house was just 1,000 sq. ft. I had made the rudimentary floor plans, and it wasn't long before we realized how small it was. The three bedrooms were barely large enough to hold a bed and dresser, and the closets were tiny. The Master Bedroom could accommodate a double, but forget a queen or king-sized bed, and its closet was more for one person than two. As you entered by the front door, the beautiful Living Room was to your right, and it was the main feature of the house. Straight ahead, and about three feet from you, was the front closet. To your left was the Dining Room which was maybe seven feet wide and included the hallway leading to the kitchen and the bedrooms. We had a full, unfinished basement which, to save a few bucks, had been constructed with cement blocks rather than poured cement. In the basement were two pumps, one for the well; it brought water into the house, and one for the sump pump hole located beside the basement sink. That pump had a dual purpose. The washing machine water drained into the hole as did any seepage through the walls. As water collected, the pump sucked it up and sent it to the ditch on the outside edge of the property, which was maybe 50 feet from the side of the house.

We spent most of our time in the Living Room, so Luc immediately set out to put in a lovely corner fireplace. However, before doing that he had to be sure of fire-prevention regulations. It was not as simple as buying a nice Franklin Stove where the fire is contained and the heat evenly distributed throughout the room. The base was important, the distance from the wall, the heat barriers, the insulated pipe from stove to wall, heat protection as it passed through the wall, and a vertical outdoor pipe, the length of which had to be in accordance with fire safety regulations. Lots of regulations! But the finished product was picturesque. I would say that room brought us a great deal of pleasure over our five years of living there.

When we have plenty, it is difficult to understand what it can be like when you have little. Water was our huge problem. Because most of it would be surface run-off, Roy (the well-driller) suggested we have a water filter installed. So we did, at the kitchen sink but not throughout the rest of the house. The pump from the well worked quite efficiently initially. However, after a few weeks, it would clog-up. At the bottom of the pipe, which leads into the well water, is a foot valve. Its purpose is to draw water, send it up the pipe, through the pump, and into the house. It works in only one direction. The surface water collected in the 2 large cauldrons sitting on the bedrock, surrounding the well, emptied into the well, as was expected, but with it came debris...earth, sand, stone. It would build and cover the well pipe and the foot valve, stopping the water from entering the house. Sometimes we would come home at night and the basement pump would be working away to no avail, just wearing itself out. So, of course, we would have to turn it off and call Roy. This happened numerous times, in those first few months. Roy would raise then cut the pipe and reset the foot valve. That pipe kept getting shorter! Once the problem was corrected we would have to prime the pump to get it going again. However, priming consisted or pouring a bucket of water into the top of the pump to get the flow started. But if your water is at the bottom of the now corrected well, how do you fill a bucket to prime the pump? It reminds me of the silly song "There's a hole in the bucket, dear Liza, dear Liza..." The song circles around to end up stating that in order to fix the bucket the person has to have a bucket. Well, in order to get the water for priming, we needed access to the water at the bottom of the well. Of course our neighbour helped us out, but this meant, in case such a problem should arise again, we needed to be prepared and always have a bucket of water on stand-by.

A few weeks after we had moved in, my parents came to visit. All was great! Like everyone else, they loved the place. However, my dad noticed that every now-and-then the lights would flicker. We had noticed as well but never gave it a second thought. He was concerned, insisted it was not right, and that we should look into it. We called our electrician who told us to inform Hydro, so we did. Then we kind of forgot about it.

Days, maybe weeks later, one afternoon, after work, as we entered the house, we could hear the toilet flushing. It was filling and draining continuously but not with water, mud. Our whole household water system was clogged with mud. But guess what? The lights no longer flickered! It would appear that Ontario Hydro had turned the electricity off to the houses that were being serviced by the same electrical transformer, replaced the old with a more powerful new, then turned the electricity back on. This had taken place at around 11 a.m., which meant our toilet had been flushing for about five hours. Until this incident, each time the well pump had been turned off, it would not begin to feed the house water until we had primed it. This time, for some reason, when the electricity restarted, so did the pump, no priming needed, in came the water! In addition, the toilet "flusher(?)" kept triggering (I don't know how else to describe it), and four or five hours later, as the well water was depleted, mud was drawn in. It would have been better for us if the pump had reacted as expected. At least then, when the electricity returned, the pump would simply have burnt itself out in a futile attempt at getting water up from the well. It would have been easier for us to have replaced the pump than to be stuck with the mess we faced that day. Roy was becoming a familiar face, and he had to contend with the well, the pump, the water filter, and the system throughout the house. What a nightmare!

The next month or so went well. Christmas was near, and we had decided to invite friends for New Year's Eve. Fall had brought lots of rain, so we had plenty of water. We were excited about showing-off our new place. Everything was great; our tiny log cabin was a huge success, and the Living Room was large enough for entertaining a few couples. We all had a good time.

A few days after the party, suddenly, the toilet would not flush. It started filling up. Luc, being a "Jack of all trades," decided to investigate and solve the problem. He instructed me to remain in the bathroom and flush the toilet when he gave the word. Meanwhile, he went downstairs, turned off the water, positioned himself, armed with a large, green, plastic, garbage bag, under the vertical pipe that led from the toilet, and as he removed the elbow joint connecting the toilet pipe to the pipe leading into the septic tank, he yelled, "Okay! Flush!" The entire contents of the toilet rushed into the bag! Then, due to the tremendous weight and force (approx. 5 gallons of water weighing 10 pounds each), Luc lost his grip, and soiled water splashed all over him and everywhere it could reach! To make bad things worse, because nothing was going through the system, he could not even clean up. However, to the rescue...the basement sink! The well was working fine, so water could run into the house; it was the house sewage disposal that was not working. The basement sink drained into the sump pump hole and out to the ditch, so we used that sink. Solid waste, though, needed to be collected and properly discarded.

Once clean-up was complete, Luc removed the horizontal pipe that ran from the base of the toilet out to the septic tank. He then understood why our toilet had backed-up...ice. When he poked at it with the butt of his hammer, he discovered it was solid.

He contacted the company that had installed our septic system. The contractor removed the earth from on top of the tank and the tank cover. The content was frozen, and the solution could only be reached in a few months: natural Spring thaw! What? We knew that particular chemicals were put into septic tanks to aid in decomposition, and the reaction, when chemical meets sewage, would serve to maintain an above freezing temperature no matter the external weather. We could not understand why our tank froze. Well, this is what we learned: it had not been buried deep enough; this fact, in tandem with cold temperatures but little snow coverage exacerbated the problem which was caused by two events. When Hydro changed the transformers, mysteriously causing the toilet to flush continuously, the tank filled with water. Use of the toilet during our party topped it off. As a result, because we had only been there a few months, there was not enough balance between water, chemicals and feces to avoid freezing. Consequently, we had to go the entire winter without the use of our bathroom or kitchen sink.

Remember I had said Luc was a "Jack of all trades?" Well he is also a pretty good artist. At that time he had become interested in old farm milk jugs. They are about three feet high; dairy farmers poured all their daily milk collection into them then would either cart them off to market or would have them picked up. Anyway, they are no longer used, so they have become collectors' items. Luc used to paint beautiful pictures on them and sell them as decoration. People would put them in their gardens, make them into tables, or just place them somewhere in their house as a decorative attraction. Luckily we had a few of these in the basement; they became our toilet. We would keep all of our plastic milk bags, fold them around the mouth of the jug, and do our business in them, tie them up, then discard. Without telling my students why, I asked them to bring me their empty milk bags, that I had a use for them, so they did!

Mornings were the worst! Once we were up, we would rush into Cornwall to Luc's sister's place and use her facilities including, of course, her shower since we had no access to ours. At our place the best we could do was a sponge bath at the sink in the basement. Have you ever heard this line of a song: "You don't know what you've got until you lose it?" We certainly understood. I remember, one evening, after dining at my sister-in-law's, I helped with the dishes. Not only did she fill the sink with water, but she ran the water constantly as she rinsed every dish, spoon, pot! All I wanted to do was collect every drop! Unbeknownst to her, I was furious! Water was precious! How could she be so frivolous with it? But it is difficult for others to understand what you lack when they have plenty. What is so valuable to you they simply take for granted.

At the end of March the septic tank thawed. Happy Day! Luc reconnected everything; we were able to use our own facilities, so we relaxed, celebrated, made tender, sweet love, and I got pregnant. We had been married for four years.

At that time, each Spring, the school board would inform individual schools if the number of teachers allocated to their school would increase or decrease for the next school year. The number of teachers in my school, for September, 1977, was to decrease. I had the fewest years of seniority, so, at three months pregnant, I had to begin looking for a new job within the board. Any principal who would hire me would know that, come mid-December I would be off on a 17-week maternity leave. I was a permanent employee, so I would get something, but I figured that my condition would be detrimental in seeking an ideal post. I was expecting to get one of the least preferred locations, perhaps a school far from home, or worse, more than one school, whereby I would have to travel between or among. As it turned out, I got the job of my first interview, full time, and it could even prove to be permanent. It was in a small village called Monkland, north of Cornwall, a bit of a distance from our place, but I was thrilled.

Come September, I was so thankful the principal had hired me, that I worked hard, and intended to teach right up until my due date, if possible. Unfortunately, because I was so conscious of my responsibilities, I guess I became a bit stressed, and it showed in my blood pressure. It was high, and the doctor warned me that if it did not improve, he would put me in the hospital for what he called "Rest and Recuperation." Knowing there was a chance I might have to take days off for this "Rest...," I worked doubly hard preparing for it...that only helped in raising my blood pressure so, on December 1st, I entered Hotel Dieu Hospital in Cornwall, believing I was there for only a few days. I was placed in a ward with three other maternity patients. My roommates all agreed that my doctor would not be sending me home until after the birth; they were right. My maternity leave had begun, and Baby Yves was born, via C-Section on December 9th, 1977, nine days before his due date. In those days, maternity leaves were paid through Unemployment Insurance (called Employment Insurance today), and definitely did not equate to our salaries.

I had to try to make up the difference. Consequently, while I was home, in the evenings, I became a Math tutor for a young girl who lived directly across the street. Her father, Jim Carr, was an insurance adjuster who would assess the damage following a home or business disaster such as a flood or fire. Because much would have been destroyed or damaged, victims would leave behind items they could not use or fix. Jim had a room in his house in which he held many of these items. He would, at some point give or donate them to those in need. Perhaps through conversations I had with his daughter during our lessons together, he learned we had a serious water problem and whether we could afford it or not, we had to buy disposable diapers for the baby. He brought over boxes and boxes of Pampers! What a good man and neighbour he was to us!

Water problems persisted. Eventually we decided we needed to consider putting in a cistern (a holding container for rainwater). At least with this we would be able to take baths and wash clothing without worrying that we might be using too much well water. The house really was pretty small, so we discussed an extension to the front, enlarging the Dining Room and having a self-contained basement underneath it in which the water would be stored. One of our neighbours was a mason. He agreed to build the basement. He described exactly what he was going to do, he guaranteed that it would not leak and that the height of the new basement would match perfectly with the existing one; the floors in both the house and the extension would align perfectly. The second basement would be of cement blocks, have its own four walls, and he would seal it completely with the type of product they used for cement swimming pools. At one end of the basement, an access hole, high on the wall, would be created between the original basement and the cistern, and a appropriate water pump installed. In early Spring, 1978, the basement hole for the cistern was dug, carefully, since the tile bed for the septic system had to be avoided, and our mason got to work. Once the cistern was completed, deconstruction of the house wall had to begin.

At school I had become good friends with the school secretary, Shirley, so we would entertain each other with our life-stories, etc. Therefore, of course, she knew about what was happening at the Chartrand residence. When I told her about the deconstruction and rebuilding task facing my husband, she told me her husband, Richard, built houses for a living, and was a "framer." I asked her if Luc could contact him to see if he might be willing to help at our place. The call was made, and Richard readily agreed. So the two men set out on this "building" journey together. They got along famously. Luc found Richard hilarious! They laughed! You know, two guys together come out with whatever expletive is on their mind. To this day, when Luc speaks of Richard it is with a smile. He also learned a lot from him, so their association, certainly for Luc, was most positive. Years later, while putting an addition on another of our homes, Luc and Richard teamed-up again. Same result. Luc really liked the guy.

As soon as Luc and Richard had removed the Dining Room wall, it became clear that the two floors were not going to be flush. The new one was a fraction of an inch higher than the original. So, when all was complete, and a new carpet put down over the entire area, there remained a constant reminder that the two floors differed, a slight bump that ran the length of the wall that had been removed.

While most of this was very serious and pretty discouraging, every now and then we would find a reason to laugh. Working with Richard made Luc's tasks easier, and they laughed a lot. One particular day our oldest, Yves, who was only four months old at the time, made us smile, well maybe quietly laugh. You see, while Luc and Richard were cutting away the large, heavy logs with our loud chainsaw, Baby Yves took his nap. He slept right through all the noise. He totally missed the event. Ha! We couldn't believe it... not a peep!

The master plan for the rainwater was that rain would funnel through the eaves-troughs, down the vertical pipe, and into the cistern which could hold up to 5,000 gallons of water. A pump located in the basement, outside of the cistern hole would deliver the collected water to the house. To get us started, Roy connected us with a company that would deliver the water and pour it into our cement holding tank. While we watched the process from our new Dining Room window, unbeknownst to us, as the water poured into the tank, it immediately seeped through the double basement walls into our basement...all 5,000gallons. We didn't suspect anything until we heard the sump pump running. Oh Gosh! What a wonderful device! The water rushed into the sump pump hole and was sent directly out to the ditch. The pump ran continuously for hours. We were so afraid it would burn-out before it could get the job done. The basement was unfinished, so we had no fear of serious damage, maybe a few items...boxes, books. The pump never gave-out, but we did have to replace it shortly afterwards. So, thousands of dollars later, we had a larger Dining Room with a crooked floor, a useless cistern, and still an insufficient water supply. We were at a total loss as to what we could do next. We had considered drilling a new well, but Roy felt that would be futile. He said our only option, at this point, would be to have an actual, vinyl pool liner fitted to the interior of the cistern and attached such that it could not disengage.

This house was costing us so much! Teaching, at that time, was not a highly-paid profession; Luc had received his BA by 1975, so his salary had improved, but each year his job for September was tenuous and would continue to be so into the foreseeable future. I, on the other hand, was able to maintain my teaching position, but my personal educational pursuits were moving at a snail's pace, so my salary was still low for a number of years. In fact, it took me twenty years to complete my BA...one course at a time: Fall, Winter, and Summer. Throughout those years I taught every subject in every elementary level, preparing, correcting, attending classes and completing assignments. In the Summers I would sit outside of the local swimming pool while each of my children took swimming lessons, and I would study or work on my latest essay. It wasn't until December of 1992 that I finally received my BA in Psychology, with a "Cum Laude." I was pretty pleased considering the fact that learning had been spread over so many years. I might, for instance, have taken a psychology course in the Fall of one year and not gotten back to its follow-up course for the next few, and yet, I was able to recall enough substance to maintain a decent average. Luc was very proud of me.

In December, 1978, Yves' first birthday and Christmas were right around the corner. We decided we would set aside our problems until the new year, take time to celebrate our son's first year with us, and focus on happiness together, his birthday, and our first Christmas as a family.

On Christmas Eve, after returning from a family gathering, Luc went to the basement to hide a couple of Yves' gifts. He noticed that our small step-ladder was propped-up against the cistern access hole. He went to investigate. As he looked into the hole he discovered that Roy had put in the liner. We never received a bill. Never! What a Merry Christmas! It was a gift that kept on giving because month after month we expected a bill that never arrived. I think Roy took pity on us. He knew, better than anyone else, what we had been going through over our first two years of home ownership. We were kind of afraid to call and thank him just in case the bill had simply been an oversight and as soon as we would mention it, the bill might show up. But you see, the liner had been a suggestion, and we had not, in fact, ordered it since money was too tight for us. He had taken it upon himself to line the cistern and give us a gift. I am convinced of that.

In the Fall of 1978, Luc decided he wanted to use the 1"x4" tongue-and-groove planks that were the replacement for the flooring we did not get. He was beginning to do more and more hands-on work around the house, and he learned with each new project. So he decided to build a detached garage at the back and to the side of the house. He had some knowledge as to how to proceed. He and his friend and teaching colleague, Lucien, poured the cement slab for the floor and inserted the anchor bolts. From there Luc was on his own. I could not help because I had Yves to care for, so I just watched as building was underway. Framing for the three walls, roof trusses, and plywood covering the roof were in place and looking good when, one day after work, we came home to a surprise and shock! The whole structure was leaning drastically! It hadn't fallen; it had simply altered from a perpendicular position to about 60 degrees. Once again, the husband of one of my acquaintances, Keith, came to the rescue. Charlotte was the custodian at my school in Monkland, and her husband was a contractor. When she told him of our dilemma, he asked Luc if he had "braced" the walls, placing diagonal boards to hold each wall at 90 degree angles both horizontally and vertically; he had not...one of those learning moments I was talking about! With our neighbour's permission, Luc drove our car onto his property, attached a rope to the garage and pulled it back into position. He then braced each wall with extra boards that had been intended for the trusses. All went well after that. Whew!

Following our disastrous first winter with no toilet facilities, and in view of the fact that our well was not supplying us with enough water, Luc built an outhouse at the back of the property. On bad days we did not use it, but when it was nice, we did. There was no house behind us, only one street of about five houses to the south and east of our place, so there was no fear of embarrassment. One day, a long while after it had been constructed, we had a mini tornado, at least I think that's what it must have been because absolutely nothing had happened at the front of the house, but when I looked out the back windows I could see that the roofs and carports on a few of the houses on the back street had been torn off. Later in the day we went for a walk to view the damage. We went out our back door, across our yard to the road leading to the street in front of the houses. As we got to the edge of our property we found a toilet seat! We had been so focused on our neighbours' homes that we had not even noticed that the wind had demolished our outhouse. Oh my, we laughed at ourselves! How unobservant!

1979 was a busy year. I had become pregnant in January. My parents and two of my sisters were living in Saudi Arabia; my dad was on the second of a two-year contract, through Bell Canada, to help the Saudis set up a communications system. They were returning to Canada in the summer because one sister was getting married here, and the other needed to complete the final years of her high school in Canada since that option was not available to her in Saudi. Mom and Dad had asked us if Elizabeth could stay with us for the year, and if I could help prepare for my other sister, Peggy's, wedding which would be taking place in August, in Glen Nevis, a tiny hamlet near their North Lancaster farm. Both Luc and I agreed, but since our second child would be arriving in September, Yves, our first born, would have to move from the small baby room into the larger bedroom. Liz would need accommodation and, being a teenager, some privacy. Consequently. Luc, with Richard once again, set out to finish a section of the basement: a small rec-room and a cute little bedroom. Once done, I liked both rooms.

Besides the fact that I was thrilled at the prospect of having my little sister with me for a year, Bell was going to pay us $100 a week for keeping her. Bonus! We were going to bank that money and try drilling another well.

As the spring approached, my sister-in-law separated from her husband and asked if she and her two daughters could stay with us until they got onto their feet again. We told her they could, but to keep in mind that Liz would be occupying the basement room once she arrived.

When the 1979 school year ended, I was seven/eight months pregnant. Luc, once again, had lost his teaching position and was told he might have a place in September if he were to take a summer course in Industrial Arts in Toronto. Tuition cost us $800; that, along with travelling expenses and room and board demolished our budget. Money was so tight, and I had mouths to feed. During the week I was preparing for Liz to arrive and making wedding plans for Peg. On Fridays I would drive into town to pick my husband up at the bus stop and, at the end of the weekend, deliver him to the bus or train for his week away. One fine day a letter arrived from Luc's school board containing his cessation papers. I remember going in to the Board on his behalf to try to ascertain the full meaning of the letter and what this meant re his prospects for September. They were non-committal, so for the rest of the summer Luc attended a course, at a cost we could not afford, on the off-chance that there might be an Industrial Arts job for him come September. It was tough!

One day, as I was talking to my friend next door, we discussed one unfortunate female neighbour whose husband had lost his job. I was expressing much sympathy for her plight when my friend said, "Kathy, why are you so busy feeling sorry for others? Look at your situation! You are eight months pregnant, shortly you will be on Maternity Leave, Luc has no job, and he is in Toronto all week every week taking an expensive course that may not benefit you at all! And you're feeling sorry for others?" We just giggled, and I said that I felt optimistic.

I was right. Luc got the Industrial Arts job. What made life so difficult from the end of each school year until the beginning of the next was the waiting. Sometimes, right up until the last minute, we would just have to hold our breaths before being able to relax knowing his job was secure for one more year.

By the time my family had arrived from Saudi, my sister-in-law and her girls had left, so fourteen-year-old Liz joined us. I don't recall a lot about Peggy and John's wedding, maybe because I had so much on my mind with the birth of my second child so close, but I do know all went really well...I have pictures to prove it. Ha! Then as soon as the events passed, and my family returned overseas, we awaited the arrival of Baby Marie-Josée.

The year following Josée's birth was a good one. Liz was fun and good company. She and Yves really got along well. He loved to spend time in her room, listening to her music and bouncing on her couch, and she and I became good friends. She would keep me company as I fed the baby, and we'd just chat; she became my confidant; when I was down she would listen, and just having her there made me feel better. She was a great help around the house. I was sorry when the year was over.

The School Board closed my little village school, so once my maternity leave for Josée ended, I had nowhere to go. Because I was a permanent employee, I was placed at the top of a supply pool list. This meant, that until I was offered another position, I would receive my full pay and be the first person called to replace a teacher. Luckily, rather than numerous single-day replacements, I was given two fairly long teaching contracts. The first was a maternity leave at Williamstown Public School, and the second, for the remainder of the school year, was at Martintown Public. Both schools were in villages fairly close to our St. Andrews West location. I had no idea what would happen to me come September. Luc and I had discussed whether we wanted another child, and since we did, we decided, rather than worrying about my next teaching assignment, I would resign in June and stay home with the kids.

Around the same time I resigned, June 1980, my parents returned from Saudi, so Liz joined them, Luc had one year of teaching Industrial Arts under his belt, and another year looked promising. Near the end of each school year The Board would make up a list of available teaching positions. Because Luc was low on the Seniority List, his position had to be posted as well. However, because he was a little more "specialized" in the teaching of Industrial Arts, due to the course he had taken in Toronto, very few others would be qualified to take over his job unless, of course, he or she were willing to go to Toronto for the same course. Before the end of June it was confirmed that his teaching position was safe, for the next year at least. However, for the next few years, this became Luc's year-end routine...position redundant, posting of available jobs, hope no one with more seniority wants his job, wait for his turn to pick, then once again get his Industrial Arts job back. As if worried anticipation was not enough, because Industrial Arts was considered a non-essential subject for elementary students, each year it stood a chance of being either cancelled or the teaching hours cut. Eventually, of course, that is exactly what happened. But we did have a few comfortable years before that eventuality occurred, and by then, Luc had adequate seniority.

Although our year with Liz had been good, our water supply still was not. We had saved the money Bell had paid us for Lizzie's rent with the intention of drilling another well. Once again, Roy attempted to find us a sufficient supply of water. It cost us every penny yet yielded no better results than the first well. He removed the pipe and filled-in the hole. He had warned us, but we felt we had to try. Nearly $5,000 wasted! Considering the fact that I would not be returning to teaching in September, 1980, clearly we could have been wiser. Now we were going to be poor, thirsty, and dirty! (Good spot here for an emoji)

From September, 1980, until June, 1981, we had to survive on one salary. It did not take us long to realize that we couldn't, so I registered with both English school boards, as a supply teacher. Benoit, our third and final child, was born in May, 1981. Up until his birth we had had a wonderful babysitter for our first two children, but she had already informed us that she was not interested in caring for three babies; after all, when Ben was born, Yves was only three-and-a-half; that's a big responsibility to ask of one caregiver. We had to find someone willing to take care of three under four years-of-age, and it would have to be on an "I'll call you as I need you" basis since I had no teaching contract. As luck would have it, a neighbour, a few houses down from us, agreed to babysit at our place whenever I got called in to teach. All was fine until I hardly ever got called. Due to that fact, she began making other plans, so when I phoned her, she would not be available. Because the call to teach would arrive first, I had to make an immediate decision, and we were so poor, that I couldn't afford to say no. I would be caught in a real bind: no one to care for the kids! A few times I had to ask my parents if they could help; they did, reluctantly. On one of these occasions, I remember my mother commenting on our lack of food and milk. I acknowledged the fact and told her that that was exactly why I could not afford to say no to supply teaching. I absolutely hated it! Once they began calling, it was always for the most difficult classes and, by the end of these days, I usually had a migraine and would have to go to bed, hopefully before the nausea did its worst on me.

As I mentioned earlier, Luc and I took out our first mortgage in 1976 at an interest rate of 11 3/4%. The five-year fixed rate opened in 1981; interest rates had sky-rocketed to 21%. Our monthly mortgage payment of $350 became $500. We couldn't handle the increase. We put the house up for sale.

In 1976, we had been approved for a mortgage of $30,000; the land had cost us $2,750; wells cost us somewhere around $10,000; landfill, corrective repair of the septic system, the garage, flooring, the extension on the front of the house to accommodate the cistern, and the repeat visits from Roy to restore the foot valve at the base of the well and to replace ruined or burnt-out pumps and sump pumps cost us tens of thousands of dollars; and finally, all the little things we had not considered, which were not included in the mortgage, such as front and back decks (necessary access to the house), the driveway, and others I have since forgotten, cost us that $4,000 we borrowed from Mom. Even without exact calculations, I knew we had spent in the neighbourhood of $60,000. In 1981, we had no choice but to put it up for sale at an asking price of $44,000, and should a buyer be interested, we were legally and morally bound to divulge the fact that water was a serious problem. Despite our discouraging journey, the house itself was unique and really cute, so as luck would have it, its beauty won-over some buyers. It had taken a number of months, but by Fall of 1982, new owners were moving, in and we were moving out.

I wish I could have stayed home with my babies; we just couldn't afford it. Consequently, after Ben was born, and while I was teaching, occasionally, I began applying for teaching positions with both the English Public and Catholic school boards. I attended one interview at our St. Andrews West local school. The interview went well, but they gave the job to someone who had the specific qualifications for which they were looking. However, a couple of weeks later I received a phone call from another Catholic school in Cornwall. They were looking for someone, and during the interview, it became clear that I was the one. The principal indicated that the St. Andrews principal had highly recommended me. I began in October, 1982, teaching Kindergarten on a half-time contract.

Our St. Andrews West house had been sold, so we began looking for a new place, this time in Cornwall, and because I was once again employed, we were able to search for something similar in price to the one we were leaving. We found a lovely bungalow located amidst other similar houses of bungalows and two-storied homes. Our house was situated right next to a city park. Lovely, perfect location! And it had water! Just an aside: a year or two later, Cornwall extended the city water system to include St. Andrews West.

Luc had to make this new place ours. He had to tweak it to suit him. Two weeks before the Closing Date had even arrived, he got access to the house and overhauled the kitchen. He even tore out a wall to put in a sliding door at the back of the house which was to open to a back deck he built later, after we had moved in.

We had a neighbour on one side, but on the other was an empty lot on which stood three or four beautiful old growth White Pine trees. This was a corner lot, and across from it was the park. Truly picturesque! Because all the buildings around us were single family homes, we assumed it was zoned R1, which meant that only houses such as these were permitted in the community. However, shortly after we moved in, contractor trucks started showing up. The beautiful trees next to our property disappeared, and a tall six-plex took their place. The owner of the beautiful corner lot had applied for and been granted a zoning change.

We were not happy; our great view was blocked, and this monstrosity was all we could see. Luc immediately started saying he wanted to move to the country where he could have space.

In those days, there was a real estate hard copy publication, MLS listings (Multiple Listing Service), that pictured and described any house and land sales in the area. We got one and began to search.

From the Frying Pan into the Fire

Now Luc had spent his entire childhood in a small neighbourhood in Cornwall and had never experienced farm life. Neither, in fact, had I, until my parents purchased our acreage in North Lancaster. However, once my husband began his frequent visits to my parents' place, he got the "bug" for land. Therefore, when we moved from St. Andrews back into the city, to the disappointment of the multi-home complex that grew up beside our place, he was angry and resolved to move where he could have space! He wanted acreage, a barn, and farm animals! Consequently, eight months after moving in to our cute bungalow in Cornwall, which I loved, we moved out to a twelve-acre hobby farm near the village of Monkland, about twenty minutes north of Cornwall.

Now I have a confession to make. I'm the one who found our third house! I had been really happy with our little bungalow, but since Luc was not, I began searching the MLS Listings (today it might be called Realtor.ca) for something he might like. I found and marked some possibilities, so one day in January, as we drove past a few of them, I directed us south, down a long north-south Monkland side road where I spotted another one on my list. At the end of the road, straight ahead of us, behind a row of trees, stood what was to become our home for the next fourteen years. On first, second, and third glance, the house was truly a shack, but my husband thought the barn was great. It wasn't until we actually entered the place and heard the particulars from our Real Estate agent that we could assess the condition and determine how much repair it would require. We should have turned and run, but I think, emotionally, Luc had already committed to it. It was cheap, so we could afford to make some repairs, but the extent to which this building needed attention was beyond what we ever should have attempted, especially considering the disaster we had lived through in St. Andrews. But Luc was sold and convinced he had it all under control. Who was I to argue? Besides, he was happy!

The positive? We had plenty of water, the setting was picturesque, and yes, the barn was in good shape. The house, should have been a tear-down. It did not even front onto a road but rather stood facing a farmer's field. What we originally thought was our 400 ft. driveway turned out to be the dead end of a county road. Our 25 ft. driveway ran perpendicular to it and nearly butted-up against the side of the house. The house sat to the west of the Dead End. Our frontage, along the fence line we faced, was approximately 400 ft. South of that fence line lay our 12 acres. The property consisted of an old post-and beam, story-and-a-half house of about 800 sq.

ft., built in 1863; a large, sturdy barn containing two sections, one of stalls for animals (cows most likely) and another for hay and grain; two small buildings, one surrounding an old well that was no longer in use, and the other a chicken coup in the shape of a mini barn; about 6 or 7 acres of usable land; then, at the back of the property, around 5 acres of swamp, part of The Newington Bog, which was not to be disturbed as it was a protected natural environment.

The front door of the house opened to one main room. To the right were 2 small rooms, a tiny kitchen and dining room. To the left were the stairs going up to the second floor, and under them, to the back left, were the stairs to the old, earth basement. The main room had probably been what the family had used as their Living Room. The house was a disaster, not livable. On the upper level, mortar and plaster had separated from the ceilings and walls, and the people before us had strapped massive sheets of plastic to catch the pieces and dust as they fell. There was only a partial bathroom with no door, in a most unacceptable spot, toilet facing the top of the stairs. The walls on the second floor had slanted ceilings, consequently, in the two bedrooms that faced the front of the house, under the slant of the roof, were tiny windows that would never do. In any emergency situation there would be no escape.

Initially we had planned some minor renovations on the second floor to address these particular issues. However, we could not tear down walls, rebuild windows, and reposition a bathroom with children around. Consequently, following the closing date at our Cornwall house, in May of 1983, we accepted temporary shelter with my parents in North Lancaster. One month, max, was to be the extent of our stay. From the first day I felt like we were intruding. I had not intended my mom to be our babysitter while we were there, but I did have a half-time teaching position, so I had to get to Cornwall. Our oldest, Yves, was also finishing his year in Kindergarten in Cornwall. We were actually fortunate enough to find a babysitter who was willing to drive out to my parents' farm! Imagine! But life there was so uncomfortable for me. Luc worked all day and spent his evenings at our new house returning to us usually quite late. I could tell the kids and I were not really welcome, because every time one of my little ones would do the slightest thing, my mother would slide her glasses from the bridge of her nose and give me a stare. I wanted out of there! I found that because I felt so uncomfortable, I would lose my temper too easily with my babies. I begged my husband to take us home. He, of course, indicated it was not yet possible.

A couple of weeks into our stay at Mom and Dad's, Luc brought me to see his progress so that I could understand that moving in was not about to happen. As soon as I walked through the front door I felt like crying. The initial Reno plan had been totally revised. What was supposed to be an upstairs project had become a complete redo... he might as well have torn down the whole place because he had as much as gutted it. There was plaster dust over everything, and in the middle of what was to become our kitchen, sat our once beautiful sofa, covered in dust. Since we had not put our furniture into storage, mainly because the downstairs was not supposed to be part of the project, it all suffered the consequences. I was so discouraged! I told him, and he agreed, that the furniture would be better off in the barn under protective covering. I returned to North Lancaster, endured, held my temper, and just waited for the day we could move-in to our Monkland home.

I think we stayed at my parents' for about six weeks. In that time, Luc had gutted the whole house. He had altered the floor plan, moved the rudimentary bathroom from the top of the stairs to the back, right of the house, created two dormers for the front bedrooms and installed larger, safer windows. All the inner walls, upstairs and down had been removed. Besides the mess of broken plaster and dust, it appeared that the form of insulation used had been, I don't know what...seeds? Anyway, every wall had been stuffed with them, leaving a massive clean-up before reconstruction could begin. We discovered the house had been built in 1863 because, stuffed into the walls was part of an old newspaper from that year.

On the main floor, Luc created a large country kitchen which, initially, also served as our living area. The original, old, dark kitchen, situated at the back right of the house, became a laundry/powder room. The small room at the right front became our telephone room since it was too small for anything else.

That beautiful sofa of which I spoke earlier found its temporary home along the wall of the stairs leading up to the bedrooms. One morning, as I was sitting on the sofa with the children, a big rat scurried out from underneath, waddled fairly quickly across the kitchen, entered the laundry room, and disappeared down one of the pipes to the basement. Of course, my husband, being as skeptical as many men are when a woman describes something scary or unsettling, thought I was exaggerating the size of the rodent; I think he figured it was just a mouse. Nonetheless, he accommodated me and called in the exterminator. The fellow who came inspected the old stone walls of the basement and said that, indeed, rats had squeezed between the old stones, and the evidence was in the greasy spots they left on the stones. He spread Warfin around the area (It was legal then), but said we would probably not get to see the critter again since Warfin dehydrates them, so they have to leave dry areas in search of water. However, the following weekend, my husband called me to the basement. There, on the earth, was what remained of the rat I had seen, and Luc had to admit that it was, indeed big! So there!

Heating was a problem...there was none! My parents gave us a used space heater that Luc installed in the south-east corner of the house. It required stove oil which we kept in a tank outside. Once the space heater was turned on, the oil would drip into the base of the heater, and we would wait a moment or two then ignite it. Once going, the heat it produced was sufficient for both down and upstairs. Unfortunately, the stove pipe that went through the corner ceiling to the outside was not long enough, and every now and then a gust of wind would blow down the pipe and extinguish the flame. Such had been the case, one afternoon, when we returned home after work. Because it was late Fall, we had left the heater on low so that, on entering the house, we would not be too chilly. However, when we arrived, we discovered that the house was cold; the flame was off. Right away, Luc started it up again. What we had not realized was the fact that even though the flame was out, the oil had continued drip-drip-dripping into the fire pot all day long. Once Luc ignited the oil, the interior lit up. Within minutes the whole stove became a massive red inferno emitting loud rumbling, pulsating sounds. The entire mini furnace seemed to grow as it glowed. We were so afraid that it was going to explode! We gathered up our three kids quickly and moved to a spot on the lawn that we believed was a safe distance from possible danger. We had left the door open so that we could monitor the situation and decide if or when we could enter the house. Eventually the "angry" stove calmed, red returned to the expected black, and life returned to normal. Needless to say, we bought a new stove pipe that extended a couple of feet above the roof line.

Throughout the first year in our new, old house, my ever-busy husband continued with seemingly unending construction renovations. The kitchen was totally overhauled. Luc removed the drop ceiling to expose the original hand hewn beam. He installed v-groove knotty pine boards between each beam. Kitchen cabinets were non-existent so he had to build some and, of course, include the sink. Pine tongue and groove seemed to be the material of choice. Upper and lower cabinets formed an L-shape, and for the upper cabinet, where the two sections met, instead of having them meet perpendicularly, he constructed a beautiful, glass cabinet door on the diagonal, and it was decoratively adorned with gorgeous grape clusters etched into the glass. Again with pine, he built a buffet and hutch, table and benches; we bought a couple of chairs to closely match our design. One project ran right into the next. Once the kitchen met his approval, Luc decided to add a Dining Room on to the back of the original farmhouse. He did not pour a basement but dropped huge anchor posts deep into the ground then, once again with his friend and framing buddy, Richard, he/they got to work. By 1984 we had a beautiful, large Dining Room, an eat-in Kitchen, Laundry and Telephone Rooms, but no formal Living Room.

In 1985, Luc set out on his biggest project: to build the Living Room, include a basement and a second story, and have the septic system updated. This was to extend the house to the west. This time he did contract-out some of the tasks, in particular the basement and the septic system including the tile bed. We'd been through this before, so he was aware of the legal and practical requirements. Once the basement and septic system were complete, he brought in a contractor for the story-and-a-half building. Luc was part of the "crew" as well. The ground floor of the new section was to include a large entry hall, from the back door, a closet, stairs to the basement, and a step down into a grand Living Room with a floor to ceiling fireplace. On the floor above there would be two additional bedrooms, and the Master Bedroom was to have an en suite bathroom, toilet and sink, and sliding doors that opened to a small deck facing the back of our property. He, along with a friend who was a mason, finished off the interior of the project with a gorgeous wood fireplace. My husband's vision turned our shack into a beautiful homestead.

During construction, a couple of minor, but could have been major, accidents occurred. Once the addition was completely closed in, Luc cut through the west wall of the original building, preparing to apply all the finishing touches necessary in combining the two sections. Everything that had been on the wall he removed, and it ended up on the floor in the Telephone Room. By 1985 our youngest, Ben, had just turned four. He went through the "stuff," found an exact o-knife, and proceeded to, accidentally, slice open his eyebrow. I was maybe 10 feet away from him, doing kitchen chores, when he came crying to me. Luc and our mason friend were outside, high up, working on the chimney when I fairly frantically called him down. Now, I had assessed the situation, knew Ben needed stitches, but also knew that he had not hurt his eye. Luc, on the other hand, was beside himself. While on our way to the hospital as I held a towel over my child's bleeding face, I had to assure my husband that everything would be fine, that the wound was just to the eyebrow. When we got to the hospital, we were seen immediately. The attendant wouldn't even let us go into the examination room with our little boy. She took him from me, told us everything would be fine, and all would take only a few minutes. True to her word, a few minutes later, she brought Ben back to us, stitched and happy. She, or the doctor, had blown up a beige medical glove and tied it at the wrist. Ben had his very own balloon that looked like a hand. He was thrilled! The episode was over; all he had to do was heal, which he did, and he even earned a small scar and a life experience story.

Once construction was finished, Luc needed to build a deck. A side door from the Dining Room and the back door of the new section of the house were high enough from the ground that they needed to open onto a raised platform. So the deck became his next project. It was to be quite large since it had to serve two entries. Perhaps it was about 18 ft. X 20 ft. One day, after all the framing was complete but the deck boards had not yet been screwed on, I caught our daughter, Josée, walking along the framing planks. Before I could get to her she fell on her face, opening up the section between her nose and upper lip. This time it was my turn to be hysterical. I guess Luc was not home at the time because I drove her to the hospital. I was so afraid she had made a serious split and might end up looking like she had a hair lip. However, at the hospital, the doctor simply closed up what turned out to be a shallow cut with a few butterfly stitches, (tiny bandages). All seemed well, but then, just as I thought everything was fine, the doctor applied a bit of medical glue to help the stitches hold. Well Jose must have also scraped her nose a bit because as he put the adhesive on, she cried out. All of a sudden I was picturing a broken nose! Had she hurt herself more than we originally thought? Well, I am an emotional fainter! My fear for her then made me a patient. I had to sit down on the step Jose had used to get up onto the hospital stretcher and recover. Her nose was fine, maybe just a little scraped. I stood up and walked with my girl to the car, but when we got there, once again, I had to sit in the driver's seat, tell Jose we were just going to rest for a moment (She was fine), and I put my head back on the backrest until I felt fully recovered.

We lived on our hobby farm for over 13 years. Luc became a turkey, chicken, and pig farmer. At one point we had a couple of ducks, but the local raccoon bit off their beaks, so they couldn't survive. We had a dog and a few feral cats. And we had stories! Our fellow teachers looked forward to hearing about our latest adventures. The one that became the biggest laugh is a pig story. Luc has always been a hilarious storyteller. In fact he will often tell me to just "Shush!" and let him do the narrating.

Each year, Luc would get his piglet as soon as it could be removed from the mother. He loved these critters! Admittedly, most baby animals are pretty cute, and piglets are no exception, but knowing that in a few months "Mimi" was going to be served at our dinner table, I was not anxious to get to know her. I left the piggy-care to my husband farmer. Pigs eat a lot and grow quickly. Apparently, after about 6 months, they are ready for the butcher. As it happened, a neighbour down the road owned an abattoir and had agreed to butcher the pig once sufficiently grown. The day came, Luc put down the tailgate of his truck, set up an appropriate ramp he had constructed, and led Mimi up the plank. Not so fast! Mimi had never been out of her enclosure. She was now 6 months old and between 200 and 300 pounds. She was not ascending any plank...forget it! What a wrestle! The squeals, the groans, the swearing?! Oh My Gosh! It must have taken my husband an hour to finally get her settled in the box of the truck. The abattoir was only a few farms away; getting her out must have been less struggle, because hubby returned within fifteen or twenty minutes. In the end, we had a great laugh (at the pig's expense of course) and a new tale to tell our school colleagues.

Luc, the storyteller, had his staff in stitches! He was and still is terrific at enhancing an experience and making it thoroughly entertaining. I tend to relay stories with just the facts, but even they were worth a giggle or two, so my staff laughed but did not react with the same emotions as my husband's friends. They insisted that they wanted to witness Piggy's trip to the abattoir the next year. They did!

The following year, Luc's staff had it all planned out. They arranged a staff party at our place, on the day the pig was to be loaded on the truck. However, a couple of weeks before delivery date, "Fifi" (name of new pig) got a bit ill. The local vet put her on meds and told Luc that she could not be slaughtered while on medication; it would spoil the meat. He would have to hold off for 2 weeks until her system was clear. No problem, the staff was flexible, they decided upon a new date, brought lots of food for the occasion, and one of the teachers even brought his movie camera. He was going to film every minute of the experience, then they would all sit down, enjoy their feast, and be entertained by the rerun of Luc struggling to put Fifi on the truck. Great intentions, but here is what happened.

Because Fifi had been sick, she was docile. Luc dropped the tailgate, set up the ramp, and walked the pig up the ramp into the truck without even a hiccup. Initially everyone was disappointed, but they decided to have a good time anyway and enjoy watching the filmed event as planned. The food was placed on the table, everyone filled their plates then sat in front of the TV to, once again, see the events of the past hour or so. The teacher who had filmed it all, pushed the VHS tape into our VCR, turned it on, then sat back with the rest of us to see the finished product. It was blank! Not one minute of the plank-walk had been filmed. All we could see was the ground, swinging back and forth before our eyes. We watched for a puzzling couple of minutes before we realized what had happened.

The brilliant filmmaker, unknowingly, had forgotten to turn the camera on for filming, but then, once the pig was in the truck, he turned it "Off," or should I say "On," and filmed the ground as he and the staff walked from the barn to the house. What a day! What an experience! They all just had to laugh!

Another animal story is mine and the children's. Each summer I would drive the kids, daily, to the Moose Creek pool. Monkland, the nearest village to the location of our farm is north of Cornwall, and Moose Creek is a town a bit further still. In the morning I would take the children to swimming lessons and often, in the afternoons they would go for public swimming. The road leading from our house to Moose Creek ran, except for a few curves, fairly straight north. One fine day, as we were returning home from swimming, we discovered why Moose Creek got its name. Driving south, on a straight stretch, in a field to our right, maybe 600 feet just north of our front door, stood two gigantic moose! They were just moseying around a large tree in the middle of a big field that butted up against our property. At first we felt privileged to see an animal others might never get to see except, perhaps, in a zoo. We were so pleased and in awe. But then I realized how close they were to our house and bay window. Suddenly a bit of fear set in! What if...? Of course nothing happened, they were not interested in either us or my bay window, we never saw them again, and, as you can see here, they just became part of a unique experience for the four of us.

Although living on a hobby farm seems ideal, there were a few drawbacks. When we first moved in, the old place was infested with flies. The window at the top of the stairs, on the east side of the house, morning and night, would be covered in flies. The window was screened; occasionally we would remove the screen and send the flies out. More often we would vacuum them up. It became part of our daily routine. As the years went by the problem improved but was never solved. We were told they bred in the old attic.

I wanted to love sitting outside on our covered deck and enjoying the view and quiet, but I never could sit for long; bees and mosquitoes would not leave me alone. Even as I hung our laundry out on the clothesline (Ah country living!) I would get attacked. Once, as I was just minding my own business, a fat bumble bee, stinger first, flew right into my cheek! The nerve!

Although the farm had only cost us around $38,000 in 1983, the old part of the house, though much improved over the next couple of years, remained drafty, so our Hydro bill was huge. Luc did 90% of the manual labour involved in bringing the "shack" from unlivable to lovely; nonetheless, it had cost us tens of thousands of dollars. Financially we were not further ahead.

The house stood over 25 ft. high. Attached to the east side of it was our TV antenna; it probably reached 30 ft. It was a foot or so away from the window at the top of the stairs. The pole itself was surrounded by a square ladder-type box. In the '80s, in the country, TV reception was tricky. We could only get a few channels, and for most, the antenna had to be adjusted. Luc was the adjuster. He would climb the rungs, vice grips in hand, to the base of the antenna pole, grip and turn the pole until the TV reception for the channel we wanted to watch was satisfactory. While he was climbing, the rest of us would set up a relay. Those watching the TV would decide when the reception was good; a second person would be situated mid-way between the Living Room, where the TV sat, and the east wall. One of us would be at the window at the top of the stairs ready to relay to Luc the message as to whether he needed to keep turning or all was good. This worked well for a time, but one fine winter day, after a freezing rain event, the TV was blurry, so the antenna needed to be turned. We began our usual routine. We all took our places, Luc went out to climb the antenna rungs, and we began our relay. From the Living Room came, "Tourne, Papa! Tourne!" The relay went through the second person and to the final one at the top of the stairs. Nothing improved! We continued calling out "Tourne, Papa! Tourne!" Well this went on for a number of minutes. We were all baffled as to why there was no improvement in the TV reception. Finally, Luc came in. He had slipped, fallen on the ice, and hurt his hand. While we were yelling at him, he was suffering and calling for help from us! He lay there until he was able to get up. We felt really sorry for him, but also for ourselves. We didn't get to watch the program we wanted! Ha! Today we can look back and laugh. Immediately afterwards we bought a rotor which we connected to the antenna and placed on the TV. All we had to do was turn the nob on the top of the little machine, and magically, the antenna would find the point of good reception. Now why had we not thought of that before? Ha!

One aspect of farm living that really did appeal to me was the prospect of having a cat and dog. They could come and go as they pleased, and all we would have to do is house and feed them. As it happened, Luc and I did not agree. He did not want animals in the house at all. We did get a dog, but he made a dog house for it. A local feral cat gave birth to four adorable kittens, but we were only allowed to feed them on the front porch, so they remained wild and would come close, but not enough to touch or pet.

Every morning when we left for work and school, as we opened the front door, the dog, who was not in his dog house but rather sleeping against the door, would jump up and yelp at the four kitties sleeping with him on his warm fur. They would scatter. In the evenings when we returned, the same scenario would be repeated. The dog would act furious and chase the cats away. Hmm! But where was the mother of these kittens? Well, that's another farm story.

Luc bought maybe a dozen baby chicks or turkeys each spring. Initially he housed them in the barn, in a pen, warmed by a heat lamp. Once they no longer needed the lamp he put them into the chicken coop, the mini wooden structure that resembled a barn; it had a door and one mesh window. Well, animals such as raccoons and cats, as it turned out, were able to tear holes in the mesh. One day my husband found dead chicks and watched as Mother Cat walked away with two chicks in her mouth, two feet protruding from each side of her mouth. The next day, when she returned for another couple of bodies, my husband shot her. Hence our dog became the surrogate parent for the kittens.

I have to preface this next story with an incident that took place a few months after we moved into the farm. A man about four properties away from ours was shot and killed. The murderer, apparently sat up in a tree outside of one of his windows and took the shot from there. As far as I know, to this day, no one was ever convicted for the crime, but I could be wrong. Imagine! We had opted for this "safe" country life. Boy were we fooled!

Although the guilty cat had been terminally punished for her thievery, Luc was aware that a wandering raccoon had discovered the flock of fowl and decided they were going to be his future meals. The critter proceeded to rip away at the mesh of the coop until he finally broke through. He killed them all. Luc was furious and decided to stand watch.

One evening, while I was sitting, inside, on the love seat situated right beside a window that looked out onto the back deck, unbeknownst to me, Luc stood with his shotgun, waiting for the raccoon he was sure would eventually appear. It did, he shot, and I jumped out of my seat. I may have been young, but I could have had a heart attack! I was so angry! How dare he do that without warning me! The first thing I thought of was the murder a few houses away. He did get the raccoon (at least that one), so I guess I was just collateral damage.

Now the murder at our neighbour's house was not the only event that captured our attention in, say, that first year. When we bought the farm, Our oldest, Yves, was about 6 years-old, Josée was 4, and Benoit was 2. Almost right away Ben went to play in the sandbox in the front yard. Within minutes he came in crying because his mouth hurt. It was full of blisters. Off to the doctor we went. He gave us a prescription for the sores, but he also informed us that the sandbox had probably been contaminated by cat feces which infected our son with Herpes Simplex that he would have for the rest of his life.

Then there was the "White Van." Yep, just like in the movies! Someone was driving around in the rural area abducting little kids. Two of the young boys on our concession road were riding their bikes south toward our driveway when they noticed they were being followed by a white van. They were not the first, we had all heard the rumours of the other children, so these two young guys were pretty scared. Unfortunately, they did not know us, so instead of riding into our yard for protection, they turned left along the east-west road and tried to outrun the van. Wisely, they rode their bikes off of the road and into a wooded spot where they dumped the bikes and ran to escape. It was a great choice. The van moved on, and the boys continued toward home once they were sure they were safe. However, these stories made all parents in the area, including us, afraid of letting our little ones out of our sight. The kids had to stay on our property and ride up and down the road by our house only as far as our mailbox.

Rural mailboxes need security cameras. Because houses are so far apart, we cannot see or hear anything that is happening even as close as next door. Just as vandalism, especially graffiti, is apparent in the city, country homes and farms suffer too. For many country dwellers, their mailboxes are quite a distance from their front door. Ours was situated at the turn of the road, probably that 400 ft. from the house that I have mentioned before. At night, I'm going to say teenagers, because I'm pretty sure adults would find no pleasure in this, would drive around smashing mailboxes. The homeowner would not know until the next day since they would have been struck late at night and they would not have heard the noise. One late night, however, Luc and a buddy had just arrived at our place when they saw this car of teens about to smash our mailbox. Luc and friend hopped right back into their car and chased the culprits. They saw the car stop right in front of a neighbour's place, a few doors down from us, and one of the kids got out. Luc informed the police; they visited the home, told the parents that their child had been seen exiting the vehicle, but the parents stood by their child and denied any culpability on their son's part. The officer reported back to Luc then the case went no further. I wonder if kids like that ever grow a conscience, realize the damage they have done, and the cost for the homeowner to fix or replace what they, the vandals, have destroyed. I wonder if they have regrets or if they just continue to laugh at their past "pranks!?"

After a while, Luc let up a little on his no dog in the house rule. He amended it to no dog on the carpets rule. At that time we had Zak. Zak was a male, German Shepherd mix, and used to wander. He had been found, a few times, in Avonmore, the nearest town, visiting the "ladies," we figured. He had a collar, so each time he was brought back to us. We needed to keep him in to avoid further wandering. He knew the rule, but after a time he decided to test it a little. Once we caught him, lying down with his head on the edge of the carpet. As soon as he saw that we noticed, he immediately retreated. However, the funniest incident occurred one day when he decided to venture upstairs, where he had never been allowed, and where the floor was fully carpeted. He got as far as the upstairs hallway. I was in our bedroom, walked out, into the hall, and there he was! He froze the second we looked at each other. He couldn't move, and I was too afraid to approach him in case he would react in an unexpected manner; I wasn't going to risk being bitten just because the dog was on the carpet. I called Luc up. He lifted the dog, cradling him from front to back, all four legs dangling, no fuss, no anger, he was gone, and life went on. Needless to say, the original rule of no animals in the house was reestablished.

One day Zak disappeared. Initially we thought, once again, that he had gone after females of the species. But a couple of weeks went by and he still had not returned. Then, one day, while working outside, Luc noticed a swarm of green-coloured flies going in and out of the empty space under our Dining Room. Upon inspection he discovered where the dog had gone. He had lain under the cover of the room above and died. Luc had been trying to get rid of the rats in the barn through the use of Warfin. He figured Zak had eaten one of the dead rats and been poisoned. He buried him on the property.

After Zak, we were in no hurry for another dog. However, as it happened, a friend of ours, who lived about a kilometre away, asked us to adopt a puppy from their dog's litter. So Kitt, a female, came to live with us. Being female, we were pretty sure she would not wander as Zak had, then, once she was a bit older, we would have her spayed. Before we could, before she even turned 1, some other wandering dog must have gotten "wind" of her, and she became pregnant probably around September/October of 1992.

In 1992 we had friends who were living in Belgium, on a

secondment, for two years. They invited us to visit, so we booked our flight; we would be spending Christmas in France. We were so excited! With that in mind, we asked Mom and Dad (my parents) to celebrate an early Christmas with us on Saturday, December 12th. They did; it was nice; all went well; but at one point Mom said she'd like to relax upstairs on my comfy bedroom La-Z-Boy chair. I walked her up, she got settled, rested for a while then joined us later. After they left, a happy Christmas at home had been accomplished, so now all we had to do was look forward to our trip.

A few days later, on December 17th, my sister, Elizabeth, called. Luc answered and passed the (landline) phone to me. All she said was, "She didn't make it, Kath."

My heart began racing. "What do you mean she didn't make it? What are you telling me?" I don't know how I sounded, but my reaction made my husband jump!

"Mom's dead. A massive heart attack. Dad drove her to the hospital, but on the way she passed out, they put her on a stretcher and tried to revive her, but they couldn't. She's gone." Of course at this point we were both crying. Luc and I went to the hospital immediately and saw her as she lay on the gurney.

The next few days were so stressful and sad. We all kept kicking ourselves for not being enough aware of the true extent of Mom's illness. She was suffering from Diabetes and had a lesion on her foot that would not heal despite both doctor and nurse efforts. However, that was our focus, not her heart! Why didn't we notice those signs? She never complained, so we fooled ourselves into thinking that, other than Diabetes and the foot, she was fine. The funeral followed a couple of days later.

Because my Acheson family and I were in mourning, I realized I would not be able to go to Belgium with Luc and the kids. My dad needed support and comfort. My sister, Peggy, Dad, and I spent the next few days together, at my place, while my husband and youngsters enjoyed a wonderful European Vacation.

That week also became Kitt's delivery time. Because she had never been allowed in the house she had to find herself a secluded, protected area on the property; she chose the empty space under the back deck. It was December, and cold, so once Kitt had her litter of pups, Peggy couldn't stand the thought that the little ones might freeze, so she crawled under the deck and rescued them one-by-one; Kitt, of course, followed. I hated to defy my husband's wishes re keeping animals outside, but Peg was already carrying them into the house. We established a little area for them in the Laundry Room. There was no door, but I still had a baby gate, so we secured that into place, closing off the entry. Kitt went out, on a regular basis to do her business, and we cleaned up after the pups. When Luc and the kids returned, the kids were thrilled, but Luc wasn't too pleased about dogs taking over our Laundry Room. He was not going to send them back outside; Peggy would not even hear of that (and she would find out even if she had returned to her own home), so he had to set them up somewhere else: the new basement. Now this was fine by me. He carried each pup down to a blanket he had placed on the floor for the little canine family. There was only one problem: Kitt had never descended twelve steps. She wanted to get to her pups but didn't know how. We were kind of at a loss as to how to encourage and reassure her. Luc decided food was the answer. He put a small piece of food on each step, coaxed her down one step then the next, until she reached the bottom. Ascending was no problem and, after a bit of trickery, descending became easy as well.

The pups were really cute, so we had no problem at all finding them homes. As soon as they had all left, we took Kitt to the veterinarian to have her spayed. Months before our crazy dog had attacked a porcupine. The vet removed the quills and told us that most dogs learn their lesson after the first encounter. However, if they go back a second time, they are bound to repeat the behaviour. Well, good old Kitt went back a second time, and the day after the operation to have her spayed, she did it again! There she lay, on the vet's table, her belly all shaved and full of stitches, while the good man, once again, removed the face-full of porcupine quills. Hmmm! Clearly, someone didn't learn her lesson.

One day Kitt was not sitting at the front door when we all got home from school. She did not show up during the evening or night, nor was she there when we went off to work in the morning. She was gone. Oh we looked for her, but really we had no idea where! Eventually we figured she was either living with some other family or had somehow died. Months went by then, one evening as we were entertaining friends, one of them opened the door to the front porch and there she was! It was unbelievable! She was so skinny that her bones protruded. I was afraid that she may have broken her hip because it looked so unnatural. However, when we, once again took her to see the vet, he said that no, she had no injuries but was just malnourished, starving. It didn't take long to bring her back to her healthy self, but to this day we have no idea what happened to her. Was she caught in a deep hole from which she couldn't escape? Such a mystery! Yet she survived and, in 1996, when we sold the farm, the people who bought it wanted us to leave Kitt with them. That was an easy decision for us because she was a farm dog and would be much happier staying than moving into the city.

Luc absolutely loved living on the farm. Besides the animals, he had his vegetable garden...massive sunflowers, corn, pumpkins...so gratifying! The kids were not as satisfied. Ben, our youngest, liked the outdoors, but the other two not so much; they had no friends and nowhere to go. Therefore, once Benoit was old enough to attend high school, we sold the farm and moved into Cornwall.

I had become used to moving. While I lived with my parents we rented an apartment and a house, owned 5 houses and the farm in North Lancaster. Once I married Luc, despite the fact that, throughout our careers we lived in and around Cornwall, we moved quite a few times: from a basement apartment to my parents' farm, to another basement apartment then the upper floor of a duplex, to our first house in St. Andrews West, to Dewhurst in Cornwall, then the farm in Monkland.

As a teenager I had been interested in house designs and had bought magazines that focused on their visual appearance and floor plans. For some reason I had held on to a few of these designs. In 1996, once I knew we were going to be moving from Monkland back into Cornwall, I riffled through my collection and found my favourite. We purchased a lot on a lovely crescent, and the contractor who had built most of the homes agreed to build ours. Because Luc had improved the farm so much, we were able to get a good price for it, so we knew we would have a great down payment. Using the original image and floor plan, I drew a slightly smaller version, cutting down on a few square feet of the total size, then we committed to having our beautiful home built. Problems arose once again. The contractor gave my husband a budget for certain rooms: kitchen cupboards, baseboards, etc., but, as I knew would happen, he could not stay within it. As a result, upon completion, on Closing Date, we were presented with a hefty bill for extra costs that we had to pay immediately. We already couldn't afford our beautiful home.

In 1996 I was assigned a very difficult class. I had no assistant. I had 28 Grade 5/6 students, only about 5 girls, a few of the students were gifted, many were average, a few were remedial (meaning they needed additional help to keep up with the others), and about 6 of them were classified as educable mentally retarded (a term that would not be accepted today...academically challenged might be more acceptable?). It was tough, too tough for me. I could not meet all of their needs. This career stress along with the financial burden of the house, sent me into a depression. I had always been the one my husband relied on for financial solutions, but I couldn't solve anything at this point. I was overwhelmed. I took a long-term disability leave from teaching which lasted a year and a few months. This is the best way I can explain my emotional journey at that time:

To the Depths and Back

One incident, one instant:
Life spins out of control.
Snap! Spirit broken!
Weakness? No. Overburdened strength.
Surrender.

Energy zapped: stomach knotted.
Mental vacuum: music dies.
Escape; sleep; dream:
Comfortable; stress free.
Stay.

Social expectations:
Go through motions: pleasant facade.
Family communication:
Feel devalued, worthless;
Outside looking in.
Dreaded chores: the dishes.
Overwhelming: tears; sleep.
Self-medication: food.
Weight gains; self-esteem plummets.

Professional therapy?
Soothing, supportive.
Pills and medication?
Not effective, useless.
Solution?
From within, one step at a time.
Step one?
The dishes.
Step two?
Once the dishes no longer evoke tears.

Throughout my leave we remained in our lovely home. We even celebrated our 25th wedding anniversary while there. However, in 1998, once I was ready to return to teaching, we agreed that the expense of our place was too much. While driving around, kind of aimlessly one day, we happened upon a new community which was in the process of being built. The name of one of the streets struck me because I had taught a student by that name: "Daprat." Coincidentally, one of the contractors was busily working in the particular raised bungalow that had caught our eye. We got bold enough to enter and ask a few questions. He was most accommodating. As it turned out, he was one of the Daprat brothers, my student's dad or uncle (I don't remember which). Together they had bought the land and were constructing a crescent of houses. That very day, while talking to him, we made a verbal offer on the place, he accepted, and we took it to our lawyer. He did his due diligent search of the title and land then informed us that there was a lean on the property that extended 35 ft. onto what would be the back corner of our land, and that lean would prevent us from dropping fence posts into the ground. Furthermore, because of the lean, we would never be able to put an in-ground pool in our backyard should we ever want to. These facts had not been presented to us at the time we made our offer, so, through the lawyer, we were able to get our bungalow on Daprat for thousands of dollars less that we had originally offered. We did have to keep in mind that should we sell, at a later date, the potential buyers would have to be informed about the lean and the restrictions it imposed. We understood and agreed.

So we moved into our lovely new home. Because we had gotten the place for less than we had expected, we decided to splurge a little. The crescent was in its infancy stage of development. The other side of the crescent had not yet been started. We had a lawn in our backyard but no fence since we had not decided what we could do to side-step the lean. As a result, behind our property was a field, and beyond that, a geared to income community. Until we had bought the Daprat home we had tried to be very frugal, but because we now had a few extra dollars, we bought two comfy lounge chairs. The very first day we had them we left them outside in the backyard overnight, thinking nothing of it! They were gone in the morning! Lesson learned!

As I mentioned before, Luc needs to make each house a home; he has to put his own touch to it. On Daprat, the basement became his project. Up until this point we had never had a finished basement, but this place was perfect. The windows were fairly large, so light flowed in easily, and each was in an ideal position for a bedroom, washroom, and family room. Luc immediately got to work completing the second half of our new house: bedroom at the back, washroom between that room and the Family Room, in which he built a very professional looking bar.

Once the construction was complete, my husband hired a plasterer. This man was so interesting! He was fast and efficient, but what impressed me most was his method for doing the ceiling; he was not tall, so he worked on stilts that he secured to his legs below the knee. So fascinating! So neat!

Our finished basement was beautiful! Our son, Yves, said it was his favourite part of the house, and because his bedroom was down there, he felt like he was living in his own apartment.

When winter arrived, once again, we had water problems. The pipes in the house froze. Not again! They were in the basement, in the wall facing the road. They were connected to the city water pipeline. However, Luc was not aware of the reason for the stoppage until he disconnected house from city. The house pipe? Frozen solid. It turns out it had not been properly insulated. City pipe? Flowing freely, and with force. It quickly flooded our entire newly constructed basement. Yves was in his room when he heard Luc cry out. He had never seen his dad appear so at a loss as to what he should do. Ultimately, they had to call the city and have them turn off the water leading to our house. That, of course took time, which meant the water kept rising. One positive? At least it was clean!

Luc brought in a company that dealt with home disasters such as the one we were experiencing. They insulated the pipe, pumped out the water, brought in fans to dry out the area, removed and replaced a few inches of Gyp-rock at the bottom of each wall, applied putty along the seams, sanded 'til all added sections were flush with the rest of the walls, then painted to match. In the end they returned the basement to its original beauty. We were extremely pleased with the efficiency and results.

We lived in our Daprat home for two years. I returned to teaching: half day Kindergarten and half day Grade 7/8. The first year was fine. I had never had an assistant in my classroom before, but there was a little girl in my Kindergarten class who had many physical challenges; she needed a nurse to give her meds and feed her because she had a tiny esophagus. This lady also helped me with the other children when her youngster did not need her. Getting 4 and 5 year-olds ready to go out for Recess sometimes proved to be a bit of a challenge. She would help me zip up coats, and put on hats, mitts and boots. The next year, everyone agreed that the little girl, although old enough for Grade 1, should remain with me in Kindergarten. Therefore, once again, I had assistance. However, that year I had one particular student who, every day, lay on the floor refusing to get ready to go out. My assistant dealt with her while I helped the rest. Finally, one day, in fact the day before Christmas vacation, out of frustration, the poor lady implored me to help her. The kid refused to cooperate. I raised my voice (we had had enough) and told her to get up and get ready to go out. It happened that a parent was in the hall at the time. She went directly to the principal's office and reported me. The principal was a nice person, we spoke, he understood, but I went home and cried throughout my entire Christmas holiday. I was not going to raise my voice for any reason from then on. My Grade 7/8 class was great, no problem, they liked me and I them, but I was no longer enjoying my half-days in Kindergarten. I resigned at the end of that year, June, 2000. I retired, traded my pension in for a Life Investment Fund through the Royal Bank, and at my husband's request, we moved to Orleans in East Ottawa.

Luc decided to finish his career in Rockland, a community east of Orleans. Our two school boards had recently expanded to include counties south and east of Ottawa, so in Rockland he could maintain his seniority and nothing would disrupt his retirement date or interfere with his pension. We bought an end-unit condo in Orleans, but we were only there a few months when the condo fees rose substantially...a condominium was not going to work for us.

In 2004 we bought another house in Orleans, but only stayed there about 8 months. My husband was not happy. He said he was going through what he called "a black hole." I thought he was depressed, since I had experienced my own "black hole," so I told him we did not have to own, I would be satisfied in a rental. The house went up for sale, and we received an offer right away. They made a $2,000 deposit. Luc had frequently mentioned that he would like to live nearer to Downtown, so, with him in mind, Josée and I found us a really cute little house, steps from the Ottawa Canal. The lease was for 13 months; I used the deposit to pay for the first month's rent. Then the offer on the house fell through, and the people wanted their money back. I guess we probably could have refused since the whole reason money is put down on an offer is to prove serious intent to buy; it's what a buyer is willing to risk for the property they want. However we felt we had to honour their wishes. The problem though, was that we no longer had their deposit; it was invested in our rental. You'll never guess what I had to do! I handed Luc all the jewellery I had at that time, and he took my rings, necklaces, and earrings to the pawn shop. He was only able to get about $890 for gems that were worth much, much more. Somehow we scrounged up the rest of the down-payment and returned it to the couple. As it turned out, I ended up moving into the rented house on my own. Luc's "black hole," I later discovered, was a girlfriend; he found himself an apartment.

Thirteen months later, from my cute little house I moved into a townhouse a bit west of the city. Each of my children, over the year and many months of our separation, spent time living with me. Eventually Luc reconnected with me and wanted back into my life. Emotionally, it had been a really tough time for me. I evaluated the pros and cons of accepting my husband back into my world, and I decided our marriage of now 32 years deserved a second chance. My daughter took over the townhouse, and Luc and I moved into another apartment in the same building in which he was already living.

Luc and I had been separated for over a year but managed to find our way back to each other. Understand! Some aspects of our relationship would never be the same. Trust was destroyed and will never be as strong as it once was; and, I believe, although we do truly care for each other, a form of love, romantic love, has definitely suffered.

We stayed in the apartment until November, 2010. I had inherited a bit of money from my dad, who had passed away in 2009, so we put it down on our present house; it has truly become our home. Will we stay here? Right now my answer is "Yes!"

This life has been a long journey, and I'm still on it! I have now been with Luc for over 50 years. Throughout that time I have witnessed, in him, tremendous growth and change. Although I can never forget the hurt he caused me through his affair, I can still appreciate the talents and skills he has developed and taught himself. For these I am his greatest fan. He has proven, to me at least, that he is living an inspirational life, but you can be the judge.

Survive
or
Thrive

Dedication

This is for my husband, Luc Chartrand. A few years ago he wrote and published a novel about the neighbourhood rectangle in which he lived for the first twenty-one years of his life. He wanted it to be lighthearted and not include any details about his personal, family struggles. I want the world to know about the events that could have broken him, and the inner strength he mustered, through self and others, to not only survive what life threw at him, the challenges and tragedies, but to actually thrive despite them.

Many young people face what feels like hopelessness, so this is for them too. Perhaps Luc's journey can inspire them to find their inner strength and succeed.

Prologue

When Agnes Chartrand passed away, in Sarsfield, Ontario, she left behind her husband, Fortunat, and their seven children. Life as a single parent is difficult, but trying to farm and raise seven kids is really challenging. Therefore, perhaps in part due to this fact, Fortunat married Marie-Louise, a stepmother for the young Chartrands. Before long, Marie-Louise and Fortunat added one more child to their family, a little girl.

Marie-Louise never really bonded with her husband's children, so when each finished elementary school, at around fourteen years-of-age, she sent them out into the world to fend for themselves. Thus, at fourteen, Claude, the third oldest Chartrand offspring, set out on his life-adventure.

The Chartrands of Danis Street

I met twenty-year-old Luc in October, 1972, at the University of Ottawa, Cornwall Branch. Our lives, before this date, had been quite different. Each, I suppose, might be considered interesting, but to me, Luc's was fascinating, tragic, yet somehow inspiring. mean I could have complained about all the little ups-and-downs of events in my young years, but here was a person who had experienced so much more.

We did have something in common: our dads were ex-military men who served throughout the duration of WW2. However, my dad, Bill, had been seventeen when he signed-up with The Navy; he had to have his dad's permission. Luc's dad, Claude, was twenty-six, had a wife, and by 1941, a daughter; he joined The Army. But even in this we were a bit different because Dad was on a ship, member of a team, and despite the losses he suffered, on whole he was happy and proud to have been a naval officer. Luc's dad, on the other hand, was an infantryman, assigned as cook, but right in the thick of the land battles; according to Luc he never talked about the war at all.

Our first few conversations made us aware that we were, probably, more different than alike. Throughout my life, my family had moved every few years between Toronto and Montreal, while Luc's had resided in one city, Cornwall, on one street, Danis. Following the war, my dad earned his Bachelor of Commerce Degree, began working for Bell Canada and moved quickly up the levels (thus the frequent moves); by 1972 his income was within the top 5% of the country. Luc's dad had been ejected from his childhood home when he was only fourteen, so he had no high school education. Therefore, following the war, when he returned to Canada, his wife, and daughter, he had to find whatever job he could to support his little family. Howard Smith Paper Mill in Cornwall offered jobs, so he took one. He put money down on a modest house in an east-end community, and that is where the Chartrand Family lived and grew.

I had never even been to Cornwall before I registered for university there. It just happened that my dad, not too fond of Quebec Politics, had decided to buy a place as close to the Quebec/Ontario Border as possible. A farm in North Lancaster, Ontario drew his attention and his dollars. Cornwall is the closest city, so off I went in search of higher education. Most of the courses were held in one of the Cornwall high schools and it was there, in the cafeteria, that Luc first sat opposite me and introduced himself. Conversation seemed so easy. I could talk about his first impression of me since we have discussed all of this so often, but this story is about Luc, my fascination with his life, my perception of how he did not only survive but at that time, was even proving he had the will to thrive. I believed, even then, that he could serve as an inspiration to so many others who face difficulties and challenges or who lack the support most of us need to succeed in life.

A few years before we met, when we were both teenagers, my dad was making somewhere in the neighbourhood of $35,000 a year, Luc's was still earning well below $10,000. However, perception is such a funny thing, isn't it? What might seem pathetic or embarrassing to one person, might appear creative or resourceful to another. Because the Chartrands rarely had cash to splurge on non-essentials, Mr. C. found other ways. Very little was discarded. When their kitchen set began to break down, he used the best of it to make a picnic table. Luc said they were the first ones on the street to have a swimming pool in their backyard (more of a wading pool I imagine). His dad used wood left over from past builds or tear-downs and some kind of sealant or tar for the seams; it never leaked, well rarely. Sitting at the cafeteria table, telling me this, Luc seemed to be almost ashamed by his hand-me-down type of existence, but I was hearing with different ears. I saw his dad as a creative, resourceful man, and I quite admired him. Luc said their double-car, detached garage contained many scraps that his dad refused to discard because they might become useful at some point in the future.

From birth until I was twenty-two, when I met Luc, I had lived in 8 houses with my parents and my 5 siblings: 5 girls and 1 boy; I was the second-oldest. Most of our places were newly built, and 6 of the 8 had 4 or 5 bedrooms. Luc's family consisted of 7 people: his parents, his 3 sisters, his brother, and himself, the youngest. They began in one, modest story-and-a-half house at the north end of his street. When Luc was about 2 years-old, they moved to a similar place closer to the south end of the same street. It was around 800 sq. ft., and the upstairs was attic space. As you entered, the living, dining-kitchen area was on the left, and the 3 bedrooms were on the right. The washroom was on the left separating the Living Room from the Kitchen/Dining Room. The house remained thus until Giselle, the oldest, moved out; Luc was about 9. His dad decided to finish the attic space in order to move the children's rooms up there.

The stairs to the attic were positioned near the door of the back bedroom, on the right. Upstairs, Luc's dad laid a plank floor and covered it with linoleum; he nailed ten-test to the walls; there were 2 windows, 1 facing the street and the other facing the backyard. He split the length of the room in half : the girls' room would be at the front with the window facing the street, and the boys' room would be at the back, with their window facing the backyard. Two closets and

73

a privacy curtain would divide the rooms. The boys slept in the room at the top of the stairs, so the girls had to pass through the boys' room to get to theirs. Luc said that one advantage to that was that the girls had to go to bed first so as not to disturb their brothers.

The new construction upstairs meant that they could now reorganize the rooms downstairs. They extended the Living Room across the full entrance of the house. Luc's parents claimed the bedroom at the middle, right, and the room to the right, at the bottom of the stairs, became the Sitting Room or Den.

Claude worked full time shifts at The Mill, but as the years passed, it was hard to make ends meet, so he and Claire decided to foster children; that would contribute a few extra dollars to their tight budget. The first youngsters to arrive were a boy and a baby girl. They came separately. The boy stayed only a few months, before he received his more permanent home, but the little girl was with the Chartrands for a couple of years. Each of them bunked-in with Mom and Dad. Later, when Luc was 11 or 12, three sisters were fostered by the Chartrands. The youngest arrived first; she was the same age as Luc. On the main floor, Claude and Claire returned the Living Room to its original size and put up a curtain separating it from the room that was, once again, to become a bedroom for the young foster child. However, months later when her sisters arrived, the three girls were sent upstairs to share bedroom space with the two Chartrand girls. Luc never really bonded with these children; he felt they were intruding on his space, I guess you could say.

As an outsider, having only heard about life at the Chartrand home in the 50s/60s, I can only offer a limited, objective opinion: both money and quarters were tight. But money and space became the least of their worries during the '60s for the worst was yet to come.

Luc is not exactly sure about how old he was when some of these events took place, so for some I will approximate. The first tragic event occurred when he was in his early teens. His mom was having recurring, massive headaches. Following numerous medical tests, her doctor told her she had a brain tumour that would have to be removed. Neurological specialists were in Montreal, so it was there Claude took her for the operation that would change their lives forever. The tumour was so intrusive that the neurosurgeon could not remove it all. He took out what he could, but the prognosis for recovery was grim. From that day on, at regular intervals, Mr. C. drove Claire to see her specialist in Montreal; the best they could do was monitor the size of the tumour and/or its growth, and manage her pain. As time passed, it became evident she was declining; her balance was off, as was her memory, and she spoke less and less because she would forget the words she was trying to use to express herself. Her frustration was often, clearly overwhelming. She might only live a few months, but perhaps years! No one knew! They did know, however, that her health would decline not improve.

One night around 11:00, June, 1965, when Luc was thirteen, his mom and dad were awakened by a knock on the door. They opened it to two police officers who were assigned the dreaded task of informing Mr. And Mrs. Chartrand that their wonderful, vibrant seventeen-year-old son, Pierre, while bike-riding home after visiting his girlfriend, was hit from behind by a drunk driver. The injuries were so severe that he had to be rushed from the hospital in Cornwall to the Montreal Neurological Institute, the same place Mrs. C. had had her operation. Pierre had multiple injuries: broken bones, lacerations, three skull fractures, and he was unconscious. He remained in a coma, under watchful eyes, for forty days. He suffered irreparable physical and brain damage, so remained in Montreal for two months, until they realized there was nothing more they could do for him. Pierre was transferred to Ottawa, St. Vincent de Paul, a chronic care facility; today it is The Bruyère Centre. He was bedridden for a number of years, incapable of even rolling over; orderlies had to do that for him. Repeatedly, he developed bed sores which had to be treated.

The Chartrands never owned a new car, and the vehicle they had was not meant to be travelling regularly from Cornwall to Montreal and/or Ottawa. Occasionally, one of Claude and Claire's sons-in-law would drive, thus saving some wear-and-tear on their 1961 Pontiac. Luc does not remember visiting his brother while he was at St. Vincent de Paul. He does though, remember one attempt at a visit. The family had made the trip up together. The facility was run by the Grey Nuns, and they insisted that visitors adhere to their (modest) dress code. Luc's sisters were wearing shorts, so they were not permitted entry. As a result, the three siblings had to wait in the car.

Travelling so far so often became very tedious and expensive for Claude. What difference would it make if Pierre were to be housed in Cornwall? He was not undergoing any kind of therapy after all, and there were care facilities in Cornwall that could provide the same services he was receiving in Ottawa. Consequently, the transfer was made, and Pierre became a full-care resident at Macdonnel Memorial on Water Street. Luc remembers that Pierre remained in his bed for a couple of years before the orderlies began putting him in a wheel chair. In addition, it was around that time that Pierre finally began to talk again. Previously he had only mumbled or groaned. Thus, two years after the accident, Pierre had reached his optimum recovery...a paraplegic with extensive brain damage: very poor muscle control and painfully halting speech.

Just a side-bar: the drunk who hit Pierre had no insurance and lost his licence for 6 months. Pierre, on the other hand, served a life-sentence, belted into a wheel chair by day, and deposited into his bed each night. He lived in full care facilities for over fifty-five years, until his death, at 72, in 2019.

Mr. Chartrand was a smoker and a weekend drinker. Luc can remember that his dad, when he could afford it, would get himself a case of six beer (occasionally twelve) for the weekend. However, he never seemed worse for wear until around the mid-sixties when, unbeknownst to him, at the time, he suffered a cardiac malaise: heart palpitations, extreme perspiration, and left arm pain. Claude, like so many in those days, refused to see a doctor. Aspirin was his cure-all. He took a couple, stayed home for a day, then resumed his work routine at The Mill; after all, no work, no pay. Then, one morning, a few years later, in late June, he woke up, got out of bed, but felt unwell; he exhibited the same symptoms he had years before. He had difficulty dressing, tying his shoes, even walking; he appeared feeble and fragile. Claire called Luc for assistance. Initially, Mr. C. talked of driving himself to the hospital, but Luc said he would take him, and his mom agreed. Once there, he stayed with his dad for a while, but when Mr. C. was taken to a room to be checked, he told Luc to go ahead home, and that he would call when he was ready to be picked up. A couple of hours later the hospital, not his dad, called to speak with Mrs. Chartrand. They informed her that her husband had had a massive thrombosis and died. It was June 27th, 1969.

The weekend following his dad's passing, Lucie, the sister closest in age to Luc, got married. The wedding had been planned since Christmas and, after consultation with the priest, both families decided to proceed. Needless-to-say, it was a more sombre than festive day.

All three girls were now married, so seventeen-year-old Luc

and his mom were living together, on their own. Claire was not able to drive, and Luc had just earned his driver's licence. It became his duty to drive his mom to her appointments at the Neurological Institute in Montreal and to accompany her, every Sunday, to visit with Pierre. This became their regular routine. Family responsibility was burdensome for one so young.

While the Chartrand family was struggling through one disaster after another, Luc clung to one constant, an anchor: his neighbourhood. Here, for a time, he could kind of forget the tragedies and pressing responsibilities and feel free to be just a teenager. Although his friends had always been important to him, they were now, also, a necessary diversion and even, perhaps, a form of life-raft. Through them he was able to look beyond his present circumstances and toward future possibilities. As they each left the area to pursue higher education, Luc took steps to do the same. He didn't know, at the time, what he wanted or expected: just more: better education and a better chance at success. He didn't want to work at the Paper Mill; he wanted a "White Collar" job not a "Blue Collar" one. He applied to and was accepted at the University of Ottawa, Teachers' College (Francais). He didn't know if he wanted to be a teacher, but it was a means to an end...it got him to Ottawa with his buddies and within his budget. Teachers' College was free and a one-year program. Student grants were available to students such as Luc, Franco-Ontarians. In the 60s/70s, a university degree was not a necessary component of teaching credentials.

Throughout his year at Teachers' College, Luc experienced residence and social life throughout the week, then on the weekends he would hitchhike back to Cornwall to care for his mother and brother. Sunday nights he would return to Ottawa. Sometimes he could carpool, but often hitchhiking was his mode of transportation.

Mrs. C.'s health continued to decline, so Luc could not return to Ottawa the following September, 1972 as he had hoped; he was needed at home. So instead, he registered at the U of O branch in Cornwall. Before he had received his formal teaching credentials, he had applied for a teaching position with the French Catholic School Board in Cornwall and been accepted. He had a great job at a senior elementary school waiting for him. Then he found out that he had not passed his French course at college; he had missed by 1%. The Board could then only take him on as a supply teacher. Meanwhile, he immediately applied to retake the exam. Once again he failed; he was at a loss as to why. The rules were that after a failed retake, you were out!

It was at this point in time, and into this world of his that I entered. For this was his world. Cornwall was foreign to me...I even got lost, on my first day of class, attempting to find the school that housed our courses (no GPS back then).

As I mentioned earlier, it was October, 1972. Luc was twenty and I was twenty-two. I had already taught for three years but decided the profession was not for me. I wanted to get my university degree and move into another field; which one I did not know. That fateful day, when Luc sat across from me in the cafeteria and introduced himself, we became fast friends. Once I learned his story, for a moment, I thought he was stringing me along! When I realized it was all true, I began to see this man as a kindred spirit: compassionate, sensitive, responsible, but beyond me, a survivor! Because of these, qualities in my eyes, I fell in love.

Our courtship was short, too short, but Mrs. Chartrand was nearing her end, and Luc wanted to have her at our wedding, so in April, 1973, only six months after we met, we married. Mrs. C. was able to attend but passed away a few months later.

In 1973 both Luc and I were attending university and working in temporary jobs, so now, as a married couple, we needed more permanent positions. Although I had not wanted to, I did return to teaching. For a couple of years, Luc continued to supply teach and work at other menial-type jobs whenever he wasn't called to substitute. One evening, as we were sitting together in our apartment, I asked him if he knew what he would truly like to do. Feeling kind of defeated, he said, "Teach." We agreed that he had to find a way.

He made an appointment with the Dean of the Faculty of Education. He asked if his two failed exams could be reviewed, to see if there was some way he could learn what he had done wrong then try the test one more time. The Dean told him that his failure was one of French Grammar and the only way he could pass and receive his teaching credentials would be if he were to take an intensive French Grammar Course, offered twice a week but only in Ottawa. So Luc travelled to Ottawa, through fair weather and foul. He took the course, earned a terrific mark and his teaching diploma. I was so proud of him (I think he was too). To this day he is a grammar buff.

I'd like to say our troubles were over, that he got his sought after teaching position and permanence, but no. For many years his position would become redundant and he would have to take specialized courses in order to be eligible for an available spot. However, in so doing, he became a specialist in Special Education and Industrial Arts, and took on jobs others were not qualified to do.

Throughout these fifty years, I have had the pleasure of witnessing the growth and development of an inspirational man. Surrounded by tragedy and burdened with responsibilities in his youth, Luc did not sit back and wallow in his misfortune. He carried his responsibilities and actively pursued a successful life.

Over the years, my husband has mourned the tragedies that befell his family, and he has also suffered pangs of guilt. Today he feels guilty about what he considers a heartless reaction to the terrible news of his brother's accident because, at the time, all he could think about was the wrecked bike...it had been his! He had loaned it to Pierre. However, when we discuss the situation, he confesses that he and his brother had not been close; his brother had considered him a pest and was never interested in having him around. I had to remind him that what happened to Pierre was not his fault, that he had been a child, not capable of being fully aware and not able to instantly turn on love and remorse for someone who, just the day before, had had no use for him. Today Luc wonders if their relationship might have improved had this horrible accident not occurred, so he mourns the possibility that died that day. From the day Pierre began his altered life, housed in a variety of care facilities, until the day our family moved to Ottawa, in 2000, Luc visited his brother every Sunday. Initially he went with his mom, until she joined Pierre at MacDonnel Memorial for the final months of her life, then on his own, but most often with me. Once we moved to Ottawa, visits with Pierre were fewer due to the distance, perhaps monthly. Pangs of guilt? Oh no! Luc was a great brother to Pierre.

Luc mourns his dad's death more than anything else. Because Mr. C. worked shifts at The Mill, Luc didn't get to see his dad as often as he would have like, so when Claude was home during the day, they did things together. They went hunting and fishing; Luc said he would even follow his dad around, jumping into the back seat of the car when he went off to do errands. Luc has told me that he cannot remember his father ever losing his temper, not even when punishment might have been deserved. He often says he felt cheated at having lost his dad when he was so young. I have to agree, of course, but as we all know, Life is not fair. Yet even in this event he harbours feelings of guilt. He kicks himself for not having stayed by his dad's side. He says he should never have left him at the hospital. I disagree. No one, not even the doctors, expected Mr. Chartrand's life to end that day. You never stop grieving for those you have loved and lost; over time you simply find new ways of dealing with it. To this day, nearly 60 years after his dad's passing, Luc will still shed tears. I cry for him too.

Mrs. Chartrand suffered for approximately eight years before her brain tumour finally took her life. Luc's greatest responsibilities yet strongest feelings of guilt seem to centre around her and those years following his dad's passing. He feels guilty for not having cared for her sufficiently. I'm not really sure what he thinks he should have changed. He feels guilty for having left her and moved into Residence at Ottawa U; yet he returned every weekend to be with her and Pierre. His sisters were in Cornwall, so they were there should she have needed help. He was nineteen and wanted what other nineteen-year-olds had: fun, independence, friends, and to pursue opportunities. Was this selfish or just natural? I say natural, but then I was not surrounded by tragedy as he was, and I was not seeing his mother's decline. So he thought leaving her had been selfish on his part. If it was, well the efforts at making it all work were nothing short of heroic, in my opinion. Preparing for a career during the week and hiking back-and-forth between Ottawa and Cornwall on the weekends? You can see why, initially, I almost didn't believe his story. He appeared more hero than selfish to me.

Luc started life in a modest-income environment, in a smaller home that housed seven people and sometimes more. His parents had grade school educations. His father worked full time throughout the years at the same manufacturing company; he was "handy" and resourceful. When tragedy struck the family, as all was caving under their feet, Luc suffered as well, of course, but he also observed, learned, and kept going. He watched his dad, and taught himself to become a "jack-of-all-trades," a "Mr. Fix- it." Our farmhouse in Monkland serves as one proof. He learned from his neighbourhood friends; he pursued teaching and fulfilled his "White Collar" dream as a teacher for thirty-six years. It is because of his fondness for his childhood neighbourhood that he decided to try his hand at writing; only by doing this could others appreciate what it had meant to him and all it had to offer. His grade school teachers were the first to suggest he had talent; he is an artist. He has carried with him only one notebook from his elementary school years: a scribbler of poetry in which, on each page, he drew and coloured a beautiful picture. Today, his acrylic paintings are testimony to that talent. He takes an artist's original painting and reproduces it tweaking it to more closely fit his view or interpretation. A few examples of Luc's artwork grace the cover of my book and follow at the end.

No one could ever call Luc lazy (except when he sits down intending to relax for a moment...within minutes he's asleep) because after his years of being a "White Collar" worker, he became a "Blue Collar" one, much to his own surprise. As soon as he retired, in 2004, he accepted two separate contracts working as Administrative Assistant for two Senators on Parliament Hill. Following that, he was offered a position as a French to English interpreter at the Provincial Courthouse. Eventually he decided he wanted to open his own business, so in 2006, "Chateau Painting," took shape. Luc began painting the interiors of homes and businesses. Today, at 71 years-of-age, he is still doing it.

Throughout the years, Luc usually had a second job, hobby, or money-making plan. He has built many decks, a couple of which grew, through the customers' requests, into extensions on their houses; he painted beautiful pictures on old farmer milk cans; he made clocks; he would order the movement then design the wooden setting; he even built grandfather clocks (ordered the kits...difficult assembly) he built a deacon's bench, coat rack, table, buffet, hutch, and benches; and he did so much to improve the houses in which we have lived. He has built kitchen cupboards; opened walls to install sliding doors; on Da Pratt he finished the basement so beautifully putting in a professional-looking bar, a bedroom, bathroom, and Family Room; and in our present home he put in a door from the house to the garage, a cute window nook, and a bay window built to extend the size of the Dining Room. And all of this is minor compared to the massive rebuild of the farm in Monkland.

Not only has my husband, Luc Chartrand, survived the tragedies of his family's past, but, while still mourning his losses, he has found ways to thrive, and so it continues!

About the Author

Kathryn Acheson Chartrand started her teaching career in 1969, at 19 years-of-age. Throughout her over 30 years, she taught every subject, except French, at every elementary grade level from Kindergarten to Grade 8. While teaching, giving birth, and caring for 3 beautiful children, she pursued, over a 20-year span, 1 course at a time, higher education through the University of Ottawa. In December, 1992, she earned her BA in Psychology.

Following her retirement, her husband and she moved from Cornwall to Ottawa, Ontario. Throughout the past 14 years she has self-published 3 books: Muriel's Footprint, a compilation of poems her mother wrote over many years of her life; Isle of View Forever, Too, a true account of her parents' relationship based on her perception and opinions; and Children: Our Future Leaders, 4 short fictitious children's stories. Journey of a Lifetime is her fourth literary contribution. It is based on the wise and often unwise decisions her husband and she made throughout their years.

Printed in the United States
by Baker & Taylor Publisher Services